The Frontline Manager's Playbook

Derrick Mains

Acknowledgements

Special thanks to Annice Laws, Martin Kupper, Andrew Kolikoff, my lovely wife Tracyann Mains, and my business partner Cyndi (Crother) Laurin for your ideas, suggestions, and editing.

Introduction from the Author

The most powerful tool that humans possess is language. Without it, there is confusion. With it, nothing is impossible.

I am willing to bet that you can go into any business and find, among departments, teams, and leaders, myriad examples of differing managerial methods, contrasting definitions and diverging semantics causing chaos, confusion, frustration and, worst of all, asymmetrical outcomes.

The truth is, our leaders and managers are hired and promoted from diverse backgrounds, with dissimilar experiences, upbringing, training, and education. Some may be new leaders and others grizzled veterans—for the most part, every one of them speaks a different language and uses different methods. This asymmetry of methods and language tarnishes the overall experience of customers and employees, and prohibits companies from achieving goals.

AMP is a different approach to management; one where circumstances are managed using specific, proven tools and a common language that compound like interest—the more you use them, the bigger and better their results.

In this book, you will meet Sophia, an inexperienced manager, whose mentor exposes her to a common language and equips her with universal tools that get immediate, tangible outcomes. The result is a streamlined management process and an opportunity for her to move from just trying to "keep the wheels on" to leading both her and her team towards greater things.

Combine common language and universal tools, and NOTHING is unattainable.

Derrick Mains
Founder of AMP Systems

Chapter 1
The Diner

"Another insane Saturday!" Sophia called out as she entered the kitchen.

"Yeah, and Anna is late ... again," Miguel piped in from his spot in front of the grill.

"Again, are you kidding me? This is the second time this week! What am I going to do about her?"

"For now, you'll have to cover her section. We're slammed, and Ben looks like the lack of coffee refills might kill him."

"All right, I'll cover for her again!" Sophia stomped out of the kitchen, brewing with anger at Anna.

Sophia put on her cheerful face as she pulled up to her first table. "Morning Ben, can I get you a refill?"

"I thought you'd never ask," Ben said as he sat at the table reading his iPad. "How are you today, Sophia? Where's Anna?"

"No show again," Sophia said with more than a tad of frustration. "Second time this week. I don't think she has any idea of the chaos it causes. Ben, I'm sorry I can't chat, I need to get some of these tables cleared."

"Busboy out as well?" Ben said with a chuckle.

"Hilarious, Ben. He's in the back, washing dishes, or at least I hope he is."

"Well, good luck."

"I'll need it with this place," Sophia replied as she walked away.

"You certainly will."

Sophia rounded the corner to return the bus tray, overloaded with dirty dishes, to the kitchen and muttered under her breath, "How the hell did I get here?"

She slid the bus tray onto the stainless-steel dish table adjacent to the steaming commercial dishwasher, through which a soggy busboy was feverishly cycling racks of tableware. Sophia met his beleaguered expression with a sympathetic grin and an encouraging thumbs up, but her face clouded again as she turned away. Grabbing a handful of wet, sanitized towels from a small red bucket to wipe down the dining room tables, she began musing to herself again.

"Eight months ago, I was content waiting tables, making good tips, and going to school at night to get my MBA. This promotion to management seemed to be a path towards better pay and more fulfillment by learning how to manage the ins and outs of a working business. It might not be the business I want to run, but it's a start. I thought I would learn something. Instead,

I do all the same tasks as before, plus more, and Rich is rarely here to help. He says I am in charge, and that means I run the show, but the only thing I ever hear from him is all the things I am *not* doing.

"I do more now than I ever did, and nothing satisfies him. Something has to change."

As the chaos of breakfast subsided, Sophia decided she had a well-earned break with a piece of pie and hot coffee coming to her. She grabbed her notebook, hoping that she could steal a few minutes to look over her Strategic Communication notes for her upcoming mid-term.

As Sophia stepped out of the kitchen, Ben caught her glance and motioned her over to his table. "What's he still doing here?" she wondered to herself. She slid into the booth across from him and slumped.

"Rough day?" Ben asked.

"Every day is rough. School is good, but I sorta wish I hadn't taken this management role, at least not until I finished my MBA and knew what I was doing."

"Sorta wish? Either you do, or you don't, Sophia. Which is it?"

"Well, it's like this, Ben. I like the idea of being the manager, but there is no support and no manual on how to do this job. I feel like I am doing the same job as before but, before, I knew I was good at it. With this, I feel like a failure.

"I don't know how to be a manager, and it shows. I do understand some of the theory and practice of management from school. But, when the rubber meets the road with stuff like people calling off or just not showing up, I have no idea how to correct that. If I ask why, they shrug and either lie to me or tell me they took a 'mental health' day. They avoid doing things they don't like to do, and they don't clean up after themselves. Sometimes, I feel like 'manager' is just another word for a 'maid.'

"Rich says, 'If people don't listen, I should talk to them. If they still don't listen, fire them.'

"Fire them?! Ben, I have never fired anyone before. I don't even know how to do that. Instead, I pick up the slack for everyone else. All the while, Rich tells me I need to get more involved in the scheduling, hiring, and marketing.

"I don't even know how to do the things he expects of me, and now he wants me to do more.

"Honestly, the hiring, marketing and schedules are things I would love to do, but I don't know how. To be candid, I don't have the time.

"Sorry Ben, I know I just dumped on you, but this sucks."

Ben was unfazed by Sophia's download and replied without missing a beat, "Sophia, what type of training and coaching has Rich given you?"

"None! Well, that is not true. On the day the former manager, Ashley, up and quit, Rich pulled me aside and told me I did a great job here. He told me I had been a great worker and always showed up, so he was making me manager. $3 more per hour is a big raise, and I was excited about it. The next morning, Rich asked me to come in thirty minutes early so he could train me. He showed me how to fill out deposit slips and all the advanced functions on the register, like how to override a transaction, credit a customer … that kinda stuff."

"That's it, Sophia?" Ben asked with a not-so-surprised look on his face.

"That's it. I feel like he thinks I magically became the leader of this diner just because I was promoted. I have never reprimanded anyone, never coached anyone, and have never hired or fired anyone. Somehow, an admin password and $3 an hour miraculously makes me Elon Musk!"

"Sophia, what you are going through is not uncommon." Ben looked directly into Sophia's eyes with a seriousness that made Sophia know that she needed to listen. "Frontline managers are the most important assets of a business, yet most business owners and leaders assume that giving them a title somehow immediately makes them ready to lead. They don't hand you a playbook, nor do they train you how to lead. They don't provide the setting to practice, hone and refine management skills over time, and this leads to high turnover, frustration, and confusion on both sides. It frustrates the business owner as much as it does the new manager."

Sophia realized that she had not been given the tools she needed, and her lack of success wasn't personal, but part of a deeper trend she was just becoming aware existed. "I wish Rich had given me a playbook. It would sure help."

"You've got that notebook you always carry around, right?" Ben asked.

"Yes, I certainly do," replied Sophia. "Maybe I'll just make my own management playbook!"

Sophia looked down at her watch and realized that she had tables to manage and a restaurant to run.

"Sorry, Ben, but I better get to it. The lunch rush comes early on Saturdays, and I still need to decide what to do about Anna."

"Good luck," quipped Ben. "You'll need it."

Sophia went back to work clearing tables, sweeping floors, and getting ready for the lunch rush. At one point in the cleanup, she bussed Ben's corner table and picked up his tab, the cash, and the always-healthy tip, pushing them into her apron pocket.

Lunch came and went, and like clockwork at 3:00 p.m. sharp, Sophia turned the sign on the door from "Come in" to "Sorry." The team cleaned up and clocked out. As she settled up the receipts and got ready to count the drawer and fill out the daily deposit slip, she noticed that Ben's receipt had a big black arrow on it right beside the words he'd written: "EXTRA TIP."

Sophia flipped over the receipt to see the words.

The Adjust

Step 1 – Anna, I see you have been late two times this week.

Step 2 – The consequences of being late to you, the team, and our customers is _____

Step 3 – Help me understand why this keeps happening?

Step 4 – Moving forward, what will you do?

Sophia thought to herself, "Ben's so sweet! He literally gave me a step-by-step guide to talking to Anna. Hmm, maybe I'll try it. But for now, I need to get to the bank."

········•••●●●••••·······

"Another insane Sunday," Sophia said at the top of her voice as her morning greeting to the staff.

"Yeah, and Anna is late again," Miguel called up from the kitchen.

"Again, are you kidding me?! This is ridiculous! When she gets here, tell her to come and see me before she clocks in! I am going to rip her a new one!"

"Ohhh, Anna's in trouble," Miguel sang from the kitchen.

"Damn straight she is! I have had enough."

"Ben needs a coffee refill," someone chirped from the floor.

"I got it," said Sophia, as she put on an apron, grabbed a pot of coffee, and headed out to the floor. Sophia felt as hot as the coffee was as she, once again, filled in for Anna.

As Sophia stepped out of the kitchen, Anna came strolling in thirty minutes late.

Sophia snapped, "Anna, I want to talk to you now! Meet me in the office. I will be there in a moment!"

Shaking with anger, Sophia filled customer cups and, without even noticing, started filling Ben's.

"Sophia, you OK?"

"Oh, Ben. It's Anna again. I am done with her. She is waiting for me in the office. I think I am just going to tell her to go home. She's fired."

"Sophia, you certainly can fire Anna. However, have you ever thought about expectations?"

"Expectations? Seriously? Show up on time *is* the expectation!"

"Is it?" inquired Ben. "Have you ever told Anna that?"

"Well, no. Of course, not. She knows that, and she is likely just taking advantage."

"Did you read my note?" Ben asked.

Sophia looked flustered, "Note? No. Oh, the 'tip' on the receipt? Yeah, briefly, and thank you, but …"

"But nothing," Ben interjected. You told me yesterday you hadn't been trained to manage people. You have never fired anyone, never reprimanded anyone, and never coached anyone. Well, now is your chance."

"Sorry, Ben, but Anna needs to go. This isn't a chance to learn. It's a chance to get rid of my problem."

"Getting rid of Anna will solve your problem?" Ben asked. "Is Anna a bad worker? Is she unpleasant? Does she get it right 80%, 90% or 95% of the time?"

Sophia shifted uncomfortably, "Well, yes, but—"

"But, what?" Ben asked in a very abrupt tone. "The main problem with Anna is one thing. It is one aspect which, while annoying, if resolved would create a good employee. Instead of firing her, use my tip and talk to her. You might be surprised."

"Ben, I am sorry. I don't have time for this." Sophia said as she turned on her heels and walked back to the office. All the while, her anger turned to fear as she realized she was ill-equipped to handle the conversation that was awaiting her on the other side of the door.

"What if I fire her, and later find out she had a good excuse? Alternatively, what if she just doesn't care, or what if she quits before I can fire her? Or worse, what if she gets angry? No, I need to walk in there and fire her.

I wish I could do this via text message."

Sophia entered the office where Anna was waiting.

"Anna, sit down." Sophia said in a tone that surprised even her and reminded her of how the nuns spoke to her in her catechism classes as a young girl.

Sophia took a moment to calm her tone and proceeded. "Anna, we have worked together for, what, five months? I love how hard you work. Your customers love you, and you always greet people with a smile. Although I wish you would clean more, you mostly do a good job. However, the reality is I am sick and tired of you always being late. You just waltz in here like you don't care. You are a great worker, and I wish things were different, but you're fired."

"Fired?" Anna said in a questioning tone. "What the hell? You just told me I was a great worker and that you liked working with me. You have never complained about me showing up late. Not once. And, I am not ALWAYS late! I was late twice this week, and once was because I had car trouble. OK, big deal. I'll make it up at the end of my shift. I need this job, and you need me. Do you think being shorthanded all the time is better than me being fifteen minutes late in the morning? Think about it. You need me. Give me another chance."

Sophia softened her demeanor and felt like she may have overstepped her position, "Well, you are right. I mean, you do a good job, and I didn't know about the car trouble. I am sorry, I'm just so stressed out right now with everything happening here at work and my midterms at school. OK, fine. Just try to be on time, OK?"

"All right, boss lady. I got tips to make," Anna blurted as she walked out the office door.

As Anna left the office, Sophia slumped. "What just happened? I walked in to fire Anna, yet I feel like I got beat up. She's right in that she is a good worker. The lateness is a problem, but I wouldn't want to try to fill her shoes all the time. Maybe I'll just come in a few minutes early each day in case she is a little behind—just in case."

Sophia headed back out front to see if she could help.

"How'd it go?" Ben asked as Sophia was rushing past the table.

"Umm, don't ask, Ben. I mean, it was OK, I guess."

"You guess?" Ben asked. "I see Anna is taking tables, so you followed my advice?"

Sophia sat down. "Yeah, it kinda didn't go as expected."

"Kinda? What do you mean by kinda?"

"Well, I told her I was tired of her always being late and—"

Ben interrupted, "Always? I thought it was just a couple times."

"Well, yeah. Anna pointed out it was only a couple of times. One of the times was because of her car. I didn't know about that. Anna reminded me that if she wasn't here, I would have to cover for her all of the time, not just on the days she's running late. So, I decided to keep her on board, and she will do her best to be here on time going forward."

"OK, let me get this straight," Ben asked inquisitively. "Anna agreed to come in on time from now on, and she understands the consequences if she doesn't?"

"Um, I don't know if you could say that," Sophia replied.

"Sophia, you either can or can't say that. Which is it?"

"No, Ben, I … well, in the moment of it all, I sorta winged it. But the good news is Anna is here now, and she will try."

"I see," Ben said with a slow head nod. "Well, I'll let you get back to it."

"OK, thanks, Ben."

As the sign turned once again from "Come in" to "Sorry," Sophia counted the receipts and thought more and more about the conversation with Anna. "Does Anna know being late affects the team, our customers, and potentially her job? Did she commit to coming in on time, or will she only try? Did I manage Anna, or did she manage me?"

Sophia pulled out the receipts from her apron, and right on top was the one she had saved from yesterday with Ben's tip.

The Adjust
Step 1 – Anna, I see you have been late two times this week.
Step 2 – The consequences of being late to you, the team and our customers is _____
Step 3 – Help me understand why this keeps happening?
Step 4 – Moving forward, what will you do?

As Sophia read each step, she realized that the earlier conversation with Anna had done nothing. There were no outcomes from that conversation and no understanding of consequences. There was no commitment to improving, and Sophia never even learned why Anna was late (other than some generic "car trouble").

Sophia thought long and hard about the conversation on the train ride out to the University that evening.

She replayed the conversation over and over, thinking of how using The Adjust could have resulted in a better outcome: a feeling of winning, a feeling of leading.

Sophia knew what she had to do.

Chapter 2
The Adjust

"Another insane Monday," Sophia called out in her usual tone. "Where's Anna?"

"Late again," Miguel hollered from the kitchen.

Sophia took a deep breath and thought to herself, "Yesterday did nothing. She had a choice. I can fire her on the spot, or I can try The Adjust."

Sophia marched out to the front just as Anna entered the front door.

"Anna, I need to see you in my office now!"

"What's up, boss lady," Anna replied.

"Office," Sophia pointed down the hallway.

As the door closed, Sophia and Anna sat down.

Sophia directed her gaze at Anna. "Anna, I see you were late again. This is the fourth time in two weeks and the third time this week. Your showing up late affects not only you. It affects our customers. Everyone else on the team has to cover for you when you aren't here. When they're covering for you, they can't keep up with their own work. It puts a ton of stress on everyone, including me. The team is getting quite resentful of having to cover for you when you are late."

Sophia continued, "Anna, help me understand why you are late?"

Anna mumbled some excuse about her alarm and late night snapchats. "I am not trying to be late. I lose track of time, and then I have a hard time getting up in the morning."

Sophia heard her out and then said, "Anna, moving forward, what will you do?" Anna replied, "Be on time more often I guess?" Sophia responded, "No, I need your commitment to be here on time every day you are on the schedule. If you are unable to be on time, I will have no alternative, except to fire you. Do you understand the consequences of being late?"

"Understood," replied Anna.

Anna stepped out of the office, and Sophia took a moment to reflect.

- I see you have been late
- The consequences are …
- Help me understand
- Moving forward, I need your commitment.

Sophia thought, "That was easy. No debates. No misunderstandings. Clear and concise. Best of all, I know I got the message across, and I know Anna received it. Let's see."

"Another crazy Tuesday," Sophia called out as she entered the kitchen.

"Good morning, boss lady," quipped Anna in her always cheerful voice as she scooted out the kitchen doors with an arm full of plates.

"On time!" Sophia thought. "OK, that's something."

Sophia headed out front to see if she needed to grab a table or two. Entering the dining room, she quickly realized the benefit of having Anna there on time. There were no backups on the floor. Everything was running smoothly. Better yet, everyone seemed to be a bit more attentive, moving a bit faster, and in a better mood.

Sophia thought to herself, "Well, maybe I'll head back to the office and take a look at the schedule."

As Sophia headed back to the office, she saw Miguel was hard at work on the line.

"Miguel, how you are today?"

"Just fine, Sophia. What are you doing back here? Aren't you usually trying to handle the rush?"

"Well, today, the rush is covered. I am going to head back to the office and work on the schedule."

"Office?" Miguel asked inquisitively. "What? That's like two times in, what, a year?"

"Hilarious, Miguel," Sophia said with a bit of sarcasm.

Miguel continued, "Hey, Sophia, I want to thank you. You are doing a great job. This Anna thing had everyone upset. Waltzing in here whenever she pleased was a downer for the rest of us. It made us think no one cared, or no one was paying attention. Truth is I think we all slacked a bit more because of it. It feels different today. Anna came out yesterday and was shaken up. She told Casey that she didn't realize how much her being a few minutes late once in a while affected the place and that you told her she either needed to get on board, or you would fire her.

"Anna is paying attention now. However, truth is, we all are. Good for you."

"Well, thanks, Miguel. That is great to hear."

"Well, you know Sophia, at my last job I got a promotion to run the whole kitchen. I had to order the food, set up the specials, and lead the team. It didn't work out so well. I wanted it to, but the problem was I was in charge of all the people I'd worked with for months. When I got promoted, they didn't respect what I had to say. They just saw me as one of the guys. If I asked them to do something, they would laugh and tell me to do it. Or, they would leave it intentionally undone, so I had to do it later. After a couple of months of that, I moved on. I came here and never looked back. No way would I ever do that management gig again. I ain't cut out for that."

The impact of her actions, and the respect she had unexpectedly generated from her staff, took Sophia aback for a moment.

"Miguel, that means a lot. Truth is, until yesterday, I felt like you did. Manager was just a title. I still did the same work for a little more money, but I had more stress. Rich seemed to want more of me, yet he was never clear about what or how. Yesterday was the first time I felt like a leader. I felt like I could do this, like I could improve things."

"That's great. Well, if you are looking for something to improve, take a look at this." Miguel motioned toward the cooktop. "See this area right here on the top, Sophia? It's never hot, never the same temperature as the rest of the cooktop. When we get busy with orders, we can't use the whole thing. We can stage stuff on that warm part, but nothing will cook there. That is part of the reason we fall behind on orders during the rush. Any shot we might persuade Rich to get someone out here to fix it?"

Sophia looked shocked. "Wow, that's crazy! I didn't know that. How long has this been an issue?"

Miguel laughed, "As long as I have been here, this cooktop hasn't worked right."

"OK, I'll chat with Rich right away, Miguel. Thanks for pointing this out." Sophia headed to the office to look at the schedule and thought to herself, "Miguel has been here three years, and nearly half of his cooktop doesn't work? How come he never said anything? I need to call Rich."

·······•••●●●••·······

"Hello?"

"Hi, Rich. It's Sophia from The Diner."

"Everything OK?" Rich said with some concern.

"Sure, things here are going well. However, I do have a question for you. I was talking with Miguel, and he pointed out that almost half of his cooktop doesn't heat properly. Can we get it repaired?"

"WHAT? That issue again?" Rich said with a frustrated tone. "You need to call the repair guy."

"OK, Rich, do you have his number?"

Rich replied, "It should be on the board behind the desk. His name is Bill. Be sure to tell him I had it repaired just last year, so it should be under warranty."

"Wait, last year?" Sophia said sounding puzzled. "Miguel said it hadn't worked for as long as he has been here!"

"You kidding me?" Rich raised his voice. "I told Ashley to have the repair guy out last year. I was in the kitchen one day and gave Miguel a hard time about only using the one side of the top. He told me the other side didn't work and, as I was leaving, I told Ashley to get it fixed."

"Well, I don't believe she ever followed through on this, Rich. Let me call Bill."

"OK. And, Sophia, get this fixed. I can't even imagine how much that affects our business."

"Will do!" Sophia took the business card from the bulletin board and dialed the numbers.

"Twin Pines Repair, this is Bill."

"Hi Bill, this is Sophia over at The Diner on 6th street. We have a cooktop that is only partially working. I spoke with the owner, Rich, and he said he thought you were out last year?"

Sophia heard keys quickly typing, and Bill responded, "Ah, nope. I have no record of being out there last year. Last time we serviced that unit was four years ago."

"Oh, OK. Well, can we get something scheduled, Bill, for as soon as possible?"

"Sure," Bill said. "I actually have a guy over there in that area now, and he is finishing up a job early. OK to send him right over?"

"Sure, that would be great. Tell him to head to the kitchen and talk to Miguel."

"Will do, Sophia. Bye now." Bill hung up the phone, and Sophia went back about her business checking the schedule.

·······•••●●●●•••·······

"Stuck valve. She's working perfectly now," the repairman said as he stuck his head in the office door.

"Really? That was fast." Sophia sounded surprised.

"Yeah," the repairman replied. "Easiest fix I have had in a while."

"OK, great. So, everything is working again? And, Miguel is happy?" Sophia inquired.

"Yes, ma'am. Just tell Rich the total bill is $50 for the trip charge. No parts were needed. Let him know the office will email the invoice to him."

"OK, great. Thank you for coming so quickly," Sophia said with some relief.

"Not quick enough it seems. Miguel said that side of the cooktop had been down for years. I am sure he is exaggerating?" The repairman added extra inflection to make it sound more like a question than a statement of fact.

"No, unfortunately, he's not. It seems the problem was never reported to me or Rich."

"Oh, I see. Sorry about that."

"Yeah, me too!" said Sophia.

Sophia thought to herself, "Fifty dollars! Fifty dollars? Three years of that cooktop not working, and fifty dollars and a phone call fixed it. How much did that cooktop not working cost us?"

Sophia continued her internal dialogue and asked herself the value and lost potential of customers who got frustrated with the wait and never came back, customers who dinged us a star or two in an online review for our "great food, slow service" comments. How many extra coffee refills did we give away while waiting for food? How many times did the Manager make adjustments because the toast was cold from sitting around waiting on eggs or bacon from the grill?

Sophia let it all sink in. "Lost customers, lost time, lost tips! Heck, we even changed the sign out front to 'Great food – takes time.' Does it? Was cooking on half a cooktop the real reason food takes so long? Fifty dollars is all it took. Fifty dollars and a phone call."

········•••••●•••·······

"Happy Wednesday, Miguel!"

"Happy Wednesday to you, Sophia! Man, I have got to tell you this fixed cooktop is my dream!" Orders are flying out. We are in a groove. No more waiting around on bacon to fry. Thanks to you, Sophia."

"Excellent Miguel. I am heading out front. Is Anna …" Sophia's voice trailed off as if she were afraid of the answer.

"Sure," Miguel said as a matter of fact. "She was here early today getting silverware wrapped for the shift."

"Wait, Anna was early?" Sophia inquired not expecting an answer from Miguel. "OK, then excellent."

Sophia grabbed an apron and headed towards the floor.

"Good morning, boss lady!" Anna chirped as Sophia walked out onto the floor.

"Good morning, Anna," Sophia replied.

Anna continued without missing a beat. "Things are cooking this morning. Literally cooking! Miguel and crew are fulfilling orders so fast we are turning tables more quickly!"

"Excellent! What can I do to help?" inquired Sophia.

"Nothing. We got it out here."

As Sophia stepped back to watch the action, she thought back to just the difference the last two days had made. Exhausted, overworked, frustrated, ready to quit, ready to fire Anna, and now 48 hours later, things had made a 180-degree turn. Just then, she glimpsed something white fluttering in the corner of her eye. Ben, the regular, was waving his napkin and trying to get Sophia's attention.

Sophia grabbed some hot coffee and headed over for the refill.

"Sorry, Ben. Here you go."

"Oh, no, Sofia. I am all filled up. Anna just topped me off."

"Oh," Sophia said with a surprised look on her face.

"How are things?" Ben asked.

Sophia replied, "Better, much better."

"Grab a seat, and tell me more?"

Sophia slid into the booth.

"Sure, Ben. I took your note and used it with Anna, and it worked. But, not just with Anna. Somehow, setting the right expectations for Anna, and sharing the consequences of her actions turned into everyone waking up a little."

"That's the way it works!" Ben exclaimed.

"It?" Sophia asked as she settled into her seat.

"Accountability!" Ben bellowed. "Accountability is an invisible force that will manage on your behalf. You just gotta let her loose, and she will always do her job."

"Her?" Sophia looked confused, looking over her shoulder as if she was being watched. "Wait, I am confused."

"Sorry, Sophia. Let me step back. Growing up, did you believe in Santa Claus?" Ben probed.

"Well, of course I did," Sophia said with a laugh. "I loved him. What's he got to do with Anna? Ben, I am perplexed."

"Give me a second to show you. In the days leading up to Christmas, were you extra careful in how you behaved because of Santa?"

"I sure was!" Sophia said with excitement as she started to sing, "You better watch out, better not cry, better not pout …"

Ben interrupted Sophia's singing, "Exactly! Knowing Santa was coming and understanding what good behavior he expected allowed you to adjust your behavior to be a good girl. You knew what the consequences would be, and you avoided them because 'Santa Claus is coming to town.' Accountability works the same way, if people know exactly what is expected of them. If they see the time frame in which it is expected, and they understand the consequences, they will generally align their behavior. It's human nature. Think about it. Invisible forces managing our unseen behavior is a big part of the world around us. World religions, loyalty to our country, all of these things are modifying our actions to get us to comply and adjust our behaviors."

Sophia inquired, "Like my grandmother with her prayers? She always told me that Jesus and the Saints were watching, even when no one else was. So, behave as you would in front of them."

Ben assured Sophia, "Sure. That is an invisible force and one you can visualize standing over your shoulder watching you. Accountability is felt but not embodied. That is why sometimes I like to think about accountability as an actual employee, similar to how your grandmother thought about Jesus and the Saints. I see accountability as a 24-7-365 manager that works on your behalf."

"Yeah, but your 'her' is imaginary," Sophia said with some authority.

"And Santa isn't?" Ben replied.

"What, are you telling me Santa isn't real?" Sophia cackled, then turned serious. "OK, Ben, I see the point."

Ben continued, "Real or imagined, accountability manages unseen behavior. When you held Anna accountable, you unleashed this unseen force to work for you. Accountability then went to work for you. She—well, 'It'—is now at work here at The Diner and performing tasks you can't even see. 'It' is giving people a feeling of order, of purpose, of, well, accountability. Knowing others on the team are all held to the same standard actually raises the standard."

"It seems to have worked. Got any other tips?" Sophia asked inquisitively.

"Plenty," Ben said with a smirk. "But, first, bask in the glow of this victory for a bit."

Sophia looked as if a light bulb had just gone off. "Wait, is that what you do? I mean, you are here every morning, and we call you 'the regular.' Usually, there is a steady stream of people that stop by your table and sit down to share a cup of coffee with you. Are those people coming to you for advice, for tips?"

"Yes, they are Sophia. You see, I used to run a successful business. I sold it a few years back, and now I mentor other business owners and leaders to help them on their path to success."

Sophia looked relieved. "Whew. Honestly, we have half-joked you were a spy! People slipping in and out of your regular booth clutching onto a handful of notes as they leave."

Ben got a good laugh out of Sophia's spy comments and decided to play along. "No, not a spy—at least as far as you know. I am just someone who has had many businesses and knows how hard it can be. It has afforded me a lot of work and life lessons I can share with others."

"Well, Ben, someday I hope I can afford a mentor like you! Your advice this week changed things here. It has improved all of our lives, for sure."

"Tell you what. You are off tomorrow, right?" Ben asked.

"Yep. Every Thursday and Friday," Sophia replied.

"Class?" Ben inquired.

"Not until 4 p.m., Ben. Why?"

"Tomorrow, Sophia, buy me lunch, and I'll share some more. Deal?"

"Deal!" said Sophia. "Meet here at noon?"

Ben replied, "Let's try something else. How about Emanuel's on 11th Avenue and Broadway?"

"Works for me. See you there, Ben."

Chapter 3

Enter Adam

"Wow! This place is hopping," Sophia called out to Ben as she sat down at the high-top table closest to the kitchen.

"It sure is," Ben remarked over the hustle and bustle of a busy lunch rush. "Notice anything different about this place?"

The host interrupted, "May I take a drink order from you?"

"I'll have a sweet tea. And, for you, Sophia?"

"Same. Thanks."

Ben continued, "Like I was saying, notice anything different here than at your place?"

"Lots!" answered Sophia. "Seems like everything is running like clockwork. Everyone seems to know their role, and they are making it happen. The customers look happy, and the employees look focused. Yeah, it looks a little different from The Diner."

"It's a little different from most businesses," Ben replied.

"Yeah, but Ben, this place is bigger than ours. They likely have more money and better training. They have it all together."

"Bigger doesn't mean much." Ben spoke with authority and looked directly in Sophia's eyes as he did back at The Diner where Sophie knew to pay attention. "However, you are right. This place has a system."

"A system, like a better POS?" queried Sophia.

Ben answered, "Not like a point-of-sale system. It's more of a way of doing business. It's a shared approach to business that everyone understands."

"Is this like the accountability lesson? Is she at work here?" Sophia asked.

"Yes, for sure," Ben replied. "Accountability is part of it, but a system is more than that. Accountability is the outcome of the system. The way you dealt with the situation with Anna opened the door to accountability, and you saw the immediate impact. Eventually, that lesson will fade. Anna will forget, and the rest of the team will, too. Having a management operating system is the solution. It is a deliberate approach to management that you follow religiously."

"Like a Novena!" Sophia thundered as if she had a good story to tell.

"A Novena?" Ben asked, not completely sure where this was going.
"Here are your sweet teas," the waiter interrupted. "Are you ready to order, or would you like a few minutes?"

Ben jumped in, "The club sandwich is amazing. I'll have that."

"Me, too," said Sophia.

Sophia continued, "Yes, a Novena. My grandmother is very religious, and she prays Novenas. She gets these little books that give you a series of prayers to pray multiple times each day for a period of days or weeks. She follows the system of prayers to obtain Gracia Especial or 'special grace.' She follows the system. Is that like the system you are talking about, Ben?"

"Exactly, Sophia. Following the system provides your grandmother with an expected outcome. Her system provides her with 'special grace.' A management system provides you with the tools and framework to manage people, processes, products or services, and profits. The system gives you a focus on making management and the business more efficient and proficient."

Ben let that sink in for a second and continued, "Many businesses are under some odd impression that they need to hire the best people they can find. Those people will automatically, and somewhat magically, make the company better."

Ben expressed the next bit with the authority only someone who had 'been there, done that' could say. "That is a fallacy. It is a total fallacy to believe that people can operate at their potential if the systems and processes those people follow are inadequate."

Ben continued speaking to Sophia about business. "We hire people because of their potential. Then we blame the lack of performance on them. All the while, it is usually a result of management not having a system or tools for their people to use and follow. Just like Rich promoting you to management and expecting you to miraculously be a leader, companies devote billions of dollars to hiring the best person, and then miraculously expect them to succeed with little instruction, processes, or tools."

"Sounds like my grandmother needs to start a business!" Sophia laughed.

"Sorry, Sophia, I am not following you here."

"Novenas, Ben. Grandma could get paid for prayers. When a company hires a new person, then they could pay Grandma to pray her Novenas in the hope of a miracle success."

Ben bellowed, "Well, it would be a miracle if it worked! Certainly, only a miracle would work for many businesses. Sophia, let me introduce you to Adam. He is the manager here, and he has a great system."

Ben looked around and noticed a member of the wait staff right behind him. "Excuse me, sir. Can you see if Adam can come out to our table?"

"Right away, sir," the waiter replied.

·····•••●●●•••······

"Ben, so great to see you! It's been a few weeks," Adam exclaimed as he arrived table side. Adam was a handsome man in his late 20s or early 30s that had a presence about him of a man in charge. He looked like a man on a mission to succeed.

"Yes, it has," Ben confirmed. "Let me introduce you to my friend. Adam, this is Sophia."

"A pleasure," Adam said in a very polite tone. "Might I assume you are a mentee as well?"

Sophia replied awkwardly, "A mentee? Oh, you mean someone that meets with Ben and gets his advice? Well, not exactly. Well, yeah, kind of, um … I mean, he comes into the restaurant I manage and—"

"Ah, you run the office," Adam said with a look of surprise and acknowledgement.

Sophia continued trying to explain, "No, no, you don't understand. Um, well …"

Adam interrupted Sophia, letting her off the hook, "Ben's office is that booth in the corner, right?"

"Oh, yes. Right, right, Ben's office." Sophia laughed with an air of relief, "Yes. Yes, I run that place. Well, at least I try!"

"Great food, takes time!" Adam said with a bit of sarcasm.

"Yeah, I wonder about that," Sophia replied.

"Ha!" Adam snorted, "Well, I wasn't going to say anything, but …" Adam left the "but" open-ended to make the point that he wondered about the "takes time" part of the slogan.

"So how do you know Ben?" Sophia asked Adam.

"Ben taught me how to run this place."

Sophia nodded.

Ben interrupted, "Well Adam, let's be honest. This place had a great system in place. It just needed a little more love on the front end."

Adam countered, "True. We are a franchise, and the head office has good, tight controls on the menu, the POS, the brand, and how we run the day-to-day kitchen. That helps a lot. But when I took over, this place was still a mess. Everyone followed the processes, but there wasn't much energy or attention to detail. We all knew what to do, but no one was leading the team. There was no accountability, no desire to improve, and no pride in what we were doing. Without that, we turned many tables and got better-than-average reviews. Yet something continued to be missing. We also turned over employees as fast as we turned over customers. The average time someone worked here was less than six months."

Adam continued, "Honestly, part of the reason I am the manager is that I stuck it out. They rewarded my loyalty with a management title. However, I was clueless when it came to how to manage. The franchise told me what to manage, but not how to do it. They never showed me that part of the business."

Ben spoke up, "And much like you, Sophia, that is how I met Adam. See, this is/was my afternoon office."

Adam laughed out loud as if reminiscing on an old joke that only he knew the punchline to. "Yeah, for a long time we thought Ben was a spy. Eleven a.m. lunch meeting, twelve noon, lunch, then a one p.m. meting, and he was out the door!"

Sophia's face lit up, "Ha! We thought the same thing over at The Diner."

Adam continued, "In many ways, he was a spy. Ben was here doing business but watching all the inefficiencies. He could see all of the places where we were missing the mark. He is a natural at seeing waste and inefficiency."

"Not a natural," Ben corrected. "I just have a system. Because of that system, I am always on the lookout for inefficiency. Once you become aware of the system, you can't turn it off."

"Ahh, the system. Thank God for that," Adam said with some excitement. "Without it, I wouldn't be where I am today. Speaking of which, Ben, I have big news! The franchisor has approached me to open a new store in Southmont."

"Great! Managing two stores is a big step up!" Ben said in a congratulatory tone.

"No, Ben," Adam said very seriously, "as the Franchisee."

"Oh, Adam, that is amazing!" Ben exclaimed.

Adam continued, but now with a puffed-up chest. "Yes, I know. I am so excited. This is all part of my plan to own many stores all across the county someday!"

"I am so proud of you, Adam," Ben said with an expression that is likely reserved for fathers and sons. "We should celebrate with dinner next week."

"You are on, Ben," retorted Adam. "I am paying. Anywhere you want to go, it's on me."

"Let's book it. Text me after your shift," Ben replied. "In the meantime, would you mind giving Sophia the tour?"

"Of course," Ben said with enthusiasm. "Sophia, are you free after lunch, or is there another time?"

"After lunch would be amazing," Sophia replied.

"Ask for me, Sophia, when you finish. I will show you around."

Sophia nodded in acknowledgement.

As Adam left the table, Ben looked proud and excited to connect Adam and Sophia. Ben spoke first. "You'll learn a lot from Adam."

"Seems like he learned a lot from you, Ben."

"Could be," Ben shook his head. "The reality is I taught him that the solution was the system."

Sophia replied, "Ok, so what is this system thing you both talk about? Tell me more."

Ben retorted as if not wanting to let Sophia in on a surprise, but about ready to at the same time. "Let Adam show you after lunch. Keep this in mind—there is only chaos and order. Every business is somewhere on the spectrum in between. The closer you are to the order side of the spectrum, the more success you are bound to have. The further from it, the closer you are to … well, not existing anymore. By putting a deliberate system in place, you bring more order. The structured approach of a system produces more order and, over time, you become more and more successful. Many companies have a system of doing things, but it is not intentional. Managers will say things like, 'that's the way we have always done it,' instead of constantly looking to improve. These business leaders accept their place on the spectrum and feel stuck. But they aren't stuck. They slide backwards toward more chaos and eventually will cease to exist."

Ben continued, "Look around at every successful company out there. They all have a system, a way of doing business, and an approach to the business that everyone knows. It is right in front of them each day. It is published, improved upon constantly, and followed religiously. Management in these companies is always looking to eliminate chaos and create order. The further away from order they are, the more risk they inherit."

Ben summed up his statement by saying, "A system of management is necessary if a company wants to grow, mature, and be profitable."

"Sophia," Ben asked, wondering if she was old enough to know, "are you familiar with Winston Churchill?"

"Leader of the UK in World War II? I learned about him in my history class," replied Sophia.

"Correct, Sophia. Churchill famously said, 'For the first 25 years of my life, I wanted freedom. For the next 25 years, I wanted order. For the next 25 years, I realized that order is freedom.'"

Ben continued, "Order doesn't have to feel like a prison. On the contrary, a system of management is the only thing that truly gives freedom. It allows the freedom to manage, improve, innovate, and grow. Without a system that brings order, there is only chaos."

Sophia spoke slowly, allowing herself to reflect on what Ben just said and her realization. "It feels like chaos at The Diner, or that's how it felt. It feels different now, more orderly."

Ben nodded and then said, "Speaking of orders, ours is here!"

· · · · · · • • ● • • · · · · · ·

Adam opened the kitchen door and invited Sophia back.

Adam spoke, "So, a little background may be helpful. This is a franchise company. Are you familiar with franchises?"

"Not really," replied Sophia.

Adam continued, "In essence, it means that someone had an excellent idea for this restaurant. They created a good brand, attracted great customers, and then decided that the best way to expand would be to replicate the successful restaurant. To franchise their idea, they had to sell their idea, their successful brand, and processes to other people who wanted to own a business. A McDonald's, for example, is independently owned by someone local, yet they are part of a big corporation."

Sophia replied, "I see. So, the owner lives and works locally but has the power of the big brand behind them."

"Exactly," Adam said enthusiastically. "And to make it all work, the Franchisor, who is the person with the original idea, created a system. They built a system that produces a consistent experience in every restaurant. The system is in place so that each local store delivers the end product as precisely as it would at the original location."

Adam continued, "The people performing the processes and following the system at each location are different, so sometimes deviation, or straying from the original, can creep in. As a manager, you must manage opportunities for processes to stray and maintain the order of things to make sure the system works efficiently. You might own a beautiful car, but if it's unmaintained, eventually it will stop running. Something as simple as a simple flat tire makes a car inoperable in the same way that a bottleneck or deviation in the system could derail the whole thing. However, just having a system doesn't mean everything will work out flawlessly."

This intrigued Sophia. "What can cause the system to stop working?"

Adam paused for a moment thinking of his answer carefully. "Lots of things. Everything from the attitudes and commitment of the people, to broken machines or less-than-optimal performance of the tools they use. It could also be changes in the supply of ingredients. So, as the manager, I am performing three core functions every day. I have a note card on my computer that reminds me of them. It says, as a Frontline Manager, my jobs are to:

- Remove barriers
- Provide resources
- Develop people

Adam continued, "If I do all three every day, I know I did a great job. That is the focus on my Gemba. Sorry, Ben calls it *The Walkabout*. Has he told you about that yet?"

Sophia replied, "Well, no. He just gave me my first bit of advice last week, and it was great, almost magical."

"That's one way to put it," Adam chuckled. "What was the advice?"

Sophia gushed without taking a single breath and said, "I had an employee that was consistently late, and I wanted to fire her, but … well, I somehow failed at doing it, and Ben jumped in with some advice."

"Ahh, The Adjust!" Adam exclaimed. "Best tool out there for setting the bar for accountability. Let me guess, it not only corrected her behavior, but it—"

Sophia interrupted, "It also upped everyone's game."

"Yep," Adam acknowledged with a head nod. "That's The Adjust. Clarity in communication is so critical to being a good manager. This isn't something the Franchisor talks about. The only things they trained me to do was to add employees to the system and how to do advanced functions on the POS system."

"Wait, really?" Sophia asked almost shocked at what she just heard. "I thought that was just me! When I was promoted, Rich, the man who owns The Diner, spent all of thirty minutes with me on the register. That was it. Somehow, he assumed I was now capable to manage people and the business."

"Trust me. It's normal," Adam said wide eyed and shaking his head. "In the management hierarchy, senior management refers to us as Frontline Managers, and there isn't much invested in us in the areas of training or development."

Sophia jumped in, "Well, I want to learn how to be a great manager. As soon as I graduate, I guess I better look for an office job to learn this stuff."

"Not so fast, Sophia," Adam interjected. "It's no better there. Trust me. My cousin, Aubrey, works for an ad agency across town, and it's the same with her. She even has a degree in business and, although she has a better understanding of how to solve problems, no one had given her the tools to lead. Well, that is until she met Ben."

"Wow! An ad agency sounds very sophisticated. That would be my dream job. So, Aubrey is also a mentee of Ben's?"

Adam spoke, "She was, and I guess she still is. She met Ben when she worked for him at his last company. She worked under his system before he sold the company. I'll be happy to introduce you to her sometime if you would like. She can tell you the story. It is actually sort of sad.

"To sum it up, Ben was a busy man when he ran that company and was rarely in the office, sometimes for just an hour or two each day. He was all over town meeting with clients and partners. But things ran like clockwork. When he sold the business, everyone assumed things would stay the same. But, as Aubrey puts it, the day Ben left, something changed. It was like all of the oxygen got sucked out of the company. People went back to old habits. They slacked off, lost interest, became zombies who were mindlessly performing tasks. The place looked busy, busier than ever, but nothing truly got done. It was just a lot of meeting and email exchanges that ended in no real progress. Aubrey quit after two months, and six months later they closed the doors."

"Adam, I would love to hear her story. Can you please introduce me to Aubrey?"

"Sure, Sophia. I'll connect you after my shift."

"Thanks, Adam."

Adam continued, "OK, so, back to the tour. Did you notice anything when you first walked in the restaurant this afternoon?"

Sophia nodded.,"To be honest, I had never been here before. When I first walked in, I wasn't sure where to go. However, immediately, the host called out to me, welcoming me to Emanuel's."

Adam continued questioning, "Was there anything else the host did?"

Sophia pondered for a moment before replying, "She asked me if it was my first time here. She again welcomed me and asked if I was dining alone or with a party. When I mentioned I was meeting someone, she immediately asked the name of the party and brought me to the table."

"Anything else?" Adam inquired.

"Let me think … well, as a matter of fact, on the way to the table, she pointed out the restroom location. She also asked if I was in a rush or if I was here to celebrate a special occasion."

"Excellent!" Adam continued, "She followed our system."

Adam went on to say, "My hosts are all trained with the following processes as part of our system." Adam held up a finger as he counted off each part of the process.

1. All guests are to be greeted within 10 seconds of arrival. No exceptions.
2. If a guest appears to be here for their first time, ask them if it is their first-time dining with us. Orient them with the restroom location. If possible, try to determine if the guest is celebrating anything today.
3. During the lunch rush, always ask if the customer is in a hurry. If so, let the wait staff know to advise the customer of dishes that take longer to prepare.
4. The host always takes the initial drink order and shares it with the wait staff, along with any instructions about the customer being in a rush or celebrating for a special occasion.

"Now, Sophia, what you didn't see is the behind-the scenes part of our system.

"Within 120 seconds of the information being passed to the wait staff, non-alcoholic drinks are delivered to the table. At that time, the wait staff asks if you are prepared to order. This is a standard we use during the lunch rush. At dinner, we would offer to enter an appetizer order. Alcoholic drinks are always delivered within 4 minutes. Check-ins occur at three minutes after food is delivered. Check-ins are required for drink refills at specified intervals. At dinner, we always bring the dessert tray to the table at the end of the meal. When we hire people, we train them on our system. We set the bar on day one of employment with us. Accountability does the rest."

This concept left Sophia in a temporary state of amazement. "Wait, Adam. Do you time people?"

"Sometimes," Adam acknowledged. "However, the understanding is that we expect our customers to see our faces and have a consistent experience every single time they dine here. No lousy Yelp reviews about not getting drinks or the server ignoring them. It just doesn't happen. Everyone knows the expectations, and everyone meets them as a team. If an individual gets behind, other team members can see it and can jump in to help.

Let's say a team member drops a drink, and that dropped drink may cause missing a check-in. It's effortless for that member to ask another team member to drop in and check on a table or two or to stop by a table awaiting drinks and offer an apology for the delay by explaining what happened. Our people and our style are very intentional and deliberate.

"As Ben says, 'To be unclear is to be unkind.'"

"I haven't heard that yet," Sophia said while truly trying to grasp what that meant. "But it applies to the situation with Anna at my restaurant. I assumed she knew that being on time was important. But I never told her how important."

"Ahh," Adam said with a laugh, "ASSUME – it makes an ASS of U and ME."

"That is hysterical, Adam." Sophia roared with laughter. "An ASS of U and ME. Oh God, it sure does. Doesn't it?"

"Another 'Ben-ism' as I call them," Adam retorted.

Sophia replied, "I love this because it's so simple. Take The Adjsut, for example. I just write it down or memorize it, and every time I face a situation, I follow the four simple steps."

Adam interjected, "And you always get a repeatable result. If you don't deviate from the tool, management becomes easy, almost effortless. It is like the paint by numbers books we had as kids."

"I loved those," Sophia said with a big smile. "I was always so careful to stay in the lines."

"That is what a management system is." Adam continued, "It's paint by numbers. Sure, you have your style, but by staying in the lines and following the instructions, you get a beautiful result every time."

"I love that, Adam! So how many of these tools does Ben have?"

"Oh, more than I know," Adam said while wondering for himself if there was any end to the tools. "But there are ten or 15 that are very important and are the foundation of everything. Once you know and master those, you are worlds ahead of just about every other Frontline Manager out there."

"Adam, can I borrow a pen. I want to write these down."

Adam ignored the request. "Oh, I think I better let Ben give you the tools as needed. It's like any type of learning. If you just read it or write it down, it doesn't stick. You need to practice it and know how to use the tool inside and out. Ben will get you there. Pay attention and realize that everything he does is intentional. Even bringing you here was no accident. Ben is big on having those he is mentoring, mentor others. Ben intentionally brought you here today so I could show you around, and I can just about bet that Ben sees something in you he believes can help me on my journey, too."

"I love it!" Sophia exclaimed. "This is like a puzzle. I feel like I'm putting together the pieces to learn the system to make me a better leader."

"Speaking of pieces," Adam continued, "let me show you how we operate here. As a rule, the menu, recipes, POS system, employee time management, and payroll are handled through the systems the franchise provides. If this wasn't a franchise, and we didn't have all these things, it would be up to us to create them. Again, the franchise is looking for consistency. That is important to you, so everything must be well documented in the event someone quits or a new person comes in and needs to jump into the system and help."

"Ugh," Sophia said as her shoulders slumped. "Right now, my cooks know the recipes and just cook from memory."

"That's dangerous!" Adam spoke with both authority and a feeling of precariousness. "What happens if one cook leaves? What if someone decides they want to make something a little different from the other cooks? Especially today, with so many allergies and intolerances, each cook must prepare by recipe. Every meal served should look, taste, and have the same ingredients as last time.

Adam continued, "The Five Alarm Chili that one day attracts heat lovers from miles around will just as quickly turn them away if one customer posts online that your Five Alarm Chili is now mild."

"How do you get your kitchen staff always to follow the recipe?" Sophia asked, hoping for a magic bullet.

"We use another of Ben's concepts," Adam responded. "We focus on awareness first. We used to tell people to follow the process or else. Essentially, we threatened them and told them if they did not follow the process, we would fire them. For some that worked, but most people resented being told what to do or else."

Sophia interjected, "Yeah, I worked for a boss like that in high school. No, thanks. We called that place 'Cell Block B.'"

Adam nodded, "Exactly. They have to follow the instructions. Rather than demanding they do so, we make them aware of the reasons. When we train a new hire, we ask them questions like, 'Do you, or anyone you know, have allergies?' Many do. We then ask, 'Have you seen what can happen to them if exposed to the thing that makes them allergic?' Most of the time, they tell us a story about a hospital visit or a ruined holiday meal. They know the effects eating the wrong thing can have on someone who is allergic. We might also ask them about their experience in dining out, giving them a short scenario, like, 'Imagine your favorite meal you eat at a restaurant is the meal you dream about. It's a big steak, wings, or piece of pie you love and could eat until you burst. Now imagine you didn't eat all day, and you are meeting friends at that place after work. All you can think about is that juicy burger or crispy wings or flaky pie. You show up and order your favorite, and it arrives at the table soggy and tasteless. How do you feel?' Their reaction is always the same, 'That would be awful,' 'That would suck,' 'I would be so upset.'"

Adam continued, "Then we connect the dots by saying. 'Many people feel like this is their favorite place. They have a dish they just can't live without, and they think all day about coming here, kicking back with a cold drink and their favorite meal. We understand that and, because of it, we take much pride in every dish being perfect, time after time. You might think it's weird how crazy we are about consistency, but we all know what if feels like to have a bad experience, or worse, an allergic reaction. We take a ton of pride in the fact that those things don't happen here. We are fanatics about it, and not just in management. We want you to be a fanatic about it, as well. Does that make sense?'

"Sophia, when we do that, it changes the game. Now it isn't me demanding you do it. It is you being aware of why it is important and understanding that winning here at Emanuel's is about that perfect, consistent experience. The franchise book tells us how, but not why. Why is up to me, the manager."

Sophia mused, "That makes so much sense, Adam. I can't even imagine if Miguel, my head cook, left. We would be lost. He has everything in his head. He tells the others what to do and how. To be honest, sometimes our food is an experiment. I can't tell you how many times a week that I hear him asking someone to 'taste this.' If we were always producing a consistent product, it would always taste the same. Now you have me thinking. If a customer asks me if there is wheat in a dish, I have a sheet that tells me what dishes do and don't. Honestly, Rich made that sheet five years ago! Miguel may have changed the recipes since then."

Adam questioned Sophia, "Yep, and have you ever seen what can happen to someone who has an allergy to wheat and eats it by mistake?"

Sophia retorted, "Yes, I have. My little sister mistakenly ate a peanut a few years back and OH!" Sophia exclaimed as she came to the realization of what Adam just did. "I see what you did there!"

Adam laughed aloud. "Awareness works! Now, if I had told you or demanded that you go back and make sure your cooks always do it the same way, you would have listened. You might even have made a little note, but likely done nothing. Even if you did, that is not to say that Miguel would have listened. But by making you aware and creating value to your awareness of the outcome or the consequences—"

"I can take action!" Sophia exclaimed.

"As long as you can," Ben continued. "That is where Ben's tools come in. They are all about giving you the ability to take action once you are aware of the problem."

"I get it. Oh, boy, I have my work cut out for me," Sophia said as her head was swimming with the work ahead of her.

"Tell you what," Adam continued, "I only have a few more minutes today. I need to hold my after-lunch Huddle. Maybe you can stop by again next week, and I can show you more?"

"Yes, that would be great," Sophia replied. "I don't want to hold you up from your … Huddle?" Sophia asked, emphasizing it as a question.

Adam understood that Sophia was curious. "It's another one of Ben's tools. They are daily Huddles. Actually, here we do them at the start and end of each shift. It's just a time we all get together as a team for five to ten minutes and talk about the day and how we could improve it. If you want to see how it works, come along."

Sophia smiled, "Sure."

······•••●●●•••·······

"Ok, everyone. Let's get started," Adam raised his voice to get everyone's attention.

"Julia, do you want to keep time?" Adam asked of the middle-aged woman to his right.

Adam continued, "We have a guest today, Sophia, who is tagging along to see how we do our Huddles, so let's get to it. Angelo, you're first. What are you most proud of today?"

Angelo spoke, "Emma at the host station asked a couple who came in for lunch and were holding hands if it was a special occasion. It just so happened they had gotten engaged last night and were meeting for lunch to discuss wedding plans. Emma shared it with Julio, and the team in the back made them a beautiful dessert. We took it to them at the end of their meal."

"Excellent!" Adam said in a celebratory tone. "Angelo, what could we have done better today?"

Angelo continued, "Seemed the seasonal vegetable side dish was a bit inconsistent. I served one table and it was 60 percent Brussels sprouts, and the next table had mostly squash with just a few sprouts. Could we improve that?"

"Sure," Adam turned to face the group. "Kitchen staff, can you watch that more closely, please?"

A number of cooks seemed to take note of the comment and shook their heads in the affirmative.

Turning his gaze back to Angelo, Adam said, "Angelo, any barriers that you see stopping us from being the best we can be?"

"No, Adam. Nothing I can think of."

"OK, Angelo." Adam inquired, "Who will be next?"

Angelo called out, "Raven!"

Adam turned to Raven and said, "Raven, what are you most proud of today?"

"Just that I am on a great team," Raven's voice cracked. "A team always trying to help me get better. I fell a little behind today putting in an order for a demanding table. Si helped me out by checking in on two of my tables. He even grabbed drink orders and delivered them for me. I appreciated that."

"I bet the customer did as well," Adam replied. "Anything we might improve on?"

"I noticed we seemed to struggle to get drink orders back to the far corner this afternoon." Raven's expression was pained. "That was my area today, and I felt rushed trying to get drinks in the 120-second standard. Do others that have worked that area feel the same?"

"Great observation," Adam acknowledged loudly and with gratitude for Raven pointing this out. He then questioned, "Anyone else felt that way?" Adam's eyebrows shot up in surprise as hands went up all around the table. "Oh, wow. I see. I will look into improving that. Raven, was that your barrier, too?"

"Yes, Adam. The distance to the drink station made it hard to hit my goal."

Adam spoke while nodding his head, "OK, Raven. Who's next?"

· · · · · · ● ● ● ● ● · · · · · · · ·

"Well, Sophia, what did you think?"

"That was good! It felt like a team, like you all cared about each other and what happened to each other. Everyone had a chance to tell the good and the bad."

"Yeah, nothing boils over here. We get it out and work through it. The best part of The Huddle is that it gives me insights into what people are talking about and what frustrates them. It gives me my assignments to remove their barriers."

Adam continued, "Remember, front line management is about:

1. Removing barriers
2. Providing resources
3. Developing people

"From today's Huddle, I now know a shared barrier of getting drinks to the back zone faster. I also know our host, Emma, deserves to be acknowledged for her great observation. The best part is I am now aware of these things, and because I am aware—"

Sophia finished Adam's sentence, "You can use the tools to take action."

"Exactly!" Adam exclaimed.

"This is so good. My head is swimming with ideas!" Sophia extended her hand. "Thank you so much for letting me tag along today."

"Of course!" Adam shook her hand warmly. "As promised, let's do it again soon. In the meantime, I will connect you with Aubrey."

"I'd appreciate that."

Chapter 4

Aubrey

"Hi, Aubrey. Thanks for making time for me." Sophia shot out her hand and shook Aubrey's with great enthusiasm.

"Not a problem," Aubrey replied. "Come on back to my office."

As Sophia walked through hallways lined with modern art and past a huge room equipped with games, pool tables, and a bar she exclaimed, "What a cool office!"

"Yeah," Aubrey said with less excitement than Sophia expected. "Ad agencies are known for going overboard on their design and perks. They say it shows clients how creative our culture is."

"Well, it is impressive," Sophia said. "It's much more impressive than our diner."

"Oh, you mean 'the office'?" Aubrey perked up. "Are you the manager there?" Aubrey continued, "Sorry, Adam said you were connected to Ben. I just didn't realize the connection."

"Yep, that's me. I have been the manager for about eight months."

Aubrey looked for the first time as if she knew why Adam had set this up. "Let me guess, your training consisted of a different login to the system, a raise, and a pat on the back."

"Pretty much," Sophia said while vigorously shaking her head in acknowledgement. "Except, I don't remember the pat on the back part."

"It's like that everywhere," Aubrey continued. "Senior management assumes that we will just jump right in, and it doesn't always work."

"And, it makes an ass of you and me," Sophia said with a chuckle.

"Oh, you know Ben all right! Ha!" Aubrey gave Sophia a big wink. "Tell me what I can help with."

Sophia spoke with a bit of reservation. "Well, I don't know. Ben pulled me aside earlier this week and told me about The Adjust. It was, well, amazing. Literally overnight, things started to change at The Diner ... uh, the office! So, Ben took me to lunch to meet Adam. Adam gave me the tour and explained to me how the system works. He showed me how everything was deliberate. He taught me about awareness and explained why I needed to be clear. He let me sit in on a huddle. It was great! I have so many ideas. I am just not sure where to start or if this will even work at The Diner. I mean, Adam has a beautiful restaurant with fine linen and a host, whereas we serve good food at a reasonable price. I'm not sure this will work for us."

"What's the difference?" Aubrey asked. "You are still serving customers, delivering a product, providing a service in exchange for money. That is what we do here as well. Heck, that is what all businesses do."

Aubrey continued, "The system can be applied anywhere, to any business. Once you master it, you can choose your destiny. Trust me when I say that good managers are in high demand. The skills at The Diner translate into many other businesses and promotions. Learning how to do hiring, firing, leading, scheduling, inventory, processes are all things done at different types of businesses. This is the language of every business, not just restaurants."

Sophia replied, as if conceding some point to her own internal dialogue, "I guess so. I hadn't thought of that. I thought that once I finished my MBA, I would take some management job somewhere and learn how a true business works."

"The Diner is not a true business?" Aubrey spoke with authority, answering her own question. "Sure, it is. It has all the same elements as this agency. The main difference is that, instead of a consistent product, we deliver custom solutions to each customer. We replace the consistent product with a consistent process."

"I see. Do you use the same tools as I would at The Diner?"

"Of course," Aubrey affirmed. "I just used The Adjust on an employee a few weeks ago. Instead of being upset and demanding he change, I found out something that changed things."

Aubrey lowered her tone and proceeded to tell Sophia the story as if it was some sort of secret.

"This employee was one of my best, always delivered on time and with great results. However, for the last week, he had been off his game. He missed deadlines, came in late, left early, and was just not himself. I could have brought him in and read him the riot-act and demand he improve, but instead I used The Adjust.

"I sat down with him and said,

1. I see you have been coming in late, and I think we both can see your work quality is less than normal.
2. The consequence of your absence is that other members of the team have to pick up the slack. That takes them away from their own assigned projects.
3. Help me understand why this is happening.

"And that's when I found out."

"Found what?" exclaimed Sophia, as if awaiting a reveal of some murder mystery story not progressing fast enough.

Aubrey continued, "That the prior week, this employee's wife had a test." Aubrey paused and said, "Her test came back abnormal."

"Oh, no!" Sophia said with a sad tone.

"Yeah, and Sophia, the reason he was late and inattentive is that he and his wife had been going to see specialists and fighting with insurance companies to get her treatment. He didn't want to take any time off, because he is concerned he may need the time for when she is getting treatment to help her and their kids."

Sophia mumbled under her breath as she cast her gaze to the floor, "That is terrible."

"It is. But it is something I can act on." Aubrey's tone changed from dejected to empowered. "I sent him home to handle things there and contacted HR about a temporary leave. They are looking at our options to see if our insurance can help. He and I also talked about how he didn't want to let the team down, and he allowed me to share with his team that he needed a few days off because of a health scare with his wife. His team stepped up, not only to handle his work, but they created a schedule to deliver meals to his home each day. One of the team members whose kids are friends with his offered to pick the kids up at school and watch them if need be."

Aubrey continued breathlessly, "Can you imagine if I had approached this my old way? Imagine if I had fired him! How helpful would it have been to demand he never be late again? He might have quit under the pressure, and my team would have had to cover for him, anyway. Not only would that have made the situation worse for him and his family, but what if the team eventually heard the whole story? I would have felt awful. My team would have seen me as a monster. Oh, it could have been terrible. Instead, my team has come together. I have a star employee that knows that we care, and we are all rallying behind him and his wife. That is the power of the system and how The Adjust can create a culture where people feel highly accountable, but also aligned with the needs of the team and the customer."

"Great story, Aubrey," Sophia replied. "Drives the point home of why The Adjust really works. Usually it adjusts the employee but, in this instance, it gave you the opportunity to adjust things to help."

"Ben is full of stories," Aubrey continued the dialogue. "Some of his stories are from when I worked for him. Other stories he shares are from his history in corporate America."

"That's right. You worked for Ben. How was that?" Sophia inquired.

"It was amazing. I got to see what a great leader looks like in action." Aubrey stared off a bit as if reminiscing on another time in her life. "Ben used systems and tools to keep the business running efficiently, even when he wasn't there to watch over it. Ben will tell you that system and tools are the keys. Set your business up with repeatable, easy to follow systems and processes, and then empower your people to improve upon those systems. All the while, the invisible force of accountability will look over everyone's shoulder and keep them engaged."

Aubrey went on, "When Ben bought the business, we were a wreck. We were really busy. Sales were good, but every order seemed to be a problem. We either didn't deliver on time, or our quality was poor. And when we *did* get orders right the first time, it was usually the result of lots of long nights, stress, and overtime. To be honest, we all thought that was just the way business worked. That is the way we had all seen it work in our past, and this company was no different. Ben showed us that it could be different.

"Ben tools slowed us down and allowed us to think through what we were doing and why. He allowed us to question why we did things a certain way. He almost demanded we ask questions, a lot of them, and that allowed us to improve time and time again. One of the first tools Ben showed me was The Fire Map."

Sophia was astonished, "Wait what kind of business were you in where you had to deal with fires?"

"Oh, not real fires," Aubrey assured her. "Saying 'fires' is a metaphor for business challenges that cause you to drop everything and focus all of your efforts on them. Some examples might be a customer complaint, a missed deadline, an incorrectly built product, or a missed appointment. We seemed to have all of the little fires that I—well, all of us—chased all day long. We were always fighting fires, so much so it became a joke. Where's Sally? 'Fighting a fire.' 'How about Juan?' 'He had to leave the office and go visit a customer to put out a fire.'

"Our old boss bought an actual firefighter helmet and, once a month, he would award it to the person who fought the most or biggest fires. We believed that was our job as managers. We actually believed we had to make sure the place didn't burn down on our watch."

"And Ben approached it differently?" Sophia asked bluntly.

"Yes, Sophia. It was so different. At Ben's company, when fires broke out, he didn't allow us to fight them immediately. He required us to determine first why and how the fire happened and, most importantly, to mark the origin of where the fire happened on the map with a red pin. After all was said and done, we had to report back on what caused the fire, how we extinguished it, and what actions needed to be taken to ensure a fire NEVER started there again. We shared our findings with other managers so that we all could collaborate on eliminating fires before they broke out.

"I think I still have one on my iPad." Aubrey picked up her iPad, unlocked the screen and swiped through a number of screens until she exclaimed, "Yes, here it is!"

Aubrey turned her iPad to Sophia and showed her the diagram.

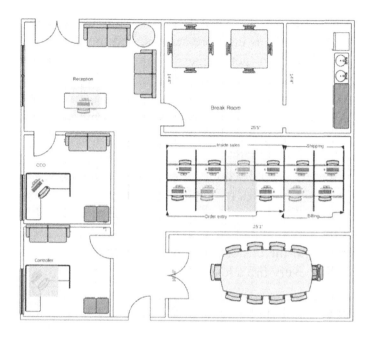

Aubrey continued explaining how she used this new tool. "I just highlighted where problems were starting, and if additional problems broke out in the same spot, I shaded it in darker. That made it really easy to visualize the origin of the fires."

Aubrey elaborated, "Let's say we repeatedly had issues with shipping defective products to our customers. In the past, we would have rushed the team to fix the problem and then rushed a new delivery to the customer with little or no testing. We'd simply cross our fingers that the new product would work. About 25% of the time, the customer received another defective product because we rushed. We wouldn't take the time to test because we were rushing to fix the problem as quickly as possible, or 'put out a fire.' When this happened, it would become even more serious, and the proverbial fire would just get bigger. Dealing with an angry customer who was losing faith and patience with us was never fun. In the end, we always satisfied the customer, but at a cost. Over time, our team's rework practices and the resentment caused by not solving the problem burned out employees. We would have to offer customers deep discounts or credits as an apology, and then offer bonuses to employees to keep them happy. We found that we not only took up far more costs to fix the problem, but we would also have to credit some amount to the customer to make up for our mistakes, making every fire a loss.

Aubrey concluded by saying, "Fire Maps helped us create a process to determine why and how crises (or fires) happened. We started getting together weekly to find a way to never have those fires again. Many times, we found that our fires concentrated around certain areas, such as sales staff over promising delivery times and project managers not being proactive enough. In some instances, we found customers started fires by not providing specifications in a timely manner, yet still expecting to get the product by the original deadline."

Sophia's head was reeling, "That is incredible! How long did it take to see results?"

"We saw results right away, but the first few weeks were frustrating and exhausting." Aubrey looked as if she was reminiscing, but this time with an uncomfortable look on her face. "Not only did we still have to fight the fires as fast as possible, but we also had to do the work to stop the fires from ever occurring again. There were lots of late nights. I felt like I dreamt about work for a month. However, for each flashpoint we eliminated, fewer fires broke out. We've solved so many causes of fires, we don't even have fire mapping meetings anymore.

Aubrey's expression changed to one of relief. "A fire breaking out is so rare now that, when it does happen, all parties involved hold a quick meeting to determine what caused it. Managers catch wind of the problem on their Walkabouts and start down the path of removing the issues that caused the fire in the first place.

"Fires are so rare now that one manager has a sign in his office saying, "384 days without S'mores!"

Sophia chuckled, "That is so funny. You just said that word again, 'Walkabout'. I think Adam called it a 'Gumbo'?"

"A Gemba, ha!" Aubrey laughed. "Ben calls it a Walkabout or in certain instances a Position to Notice, but in Japan the word is Gemba. A Walkabout is a simple walk that every manager needs to do at least twice each day. The manager simply walks through the office, the kitchen, the warehouse, the server farm, the fields, wherever the work is done, observing the work being done. Ben loves to say, 'Your answers are just thirty feet away, but you need to get off your rear and to get them.' Every day, at least twice a day, I get out of my office and I walk with no specific agenda. I intentionally walk around the office. I ask people how they are; I tell them I appreciate their work, and I ask questions about the work they're doing.

Aubrey continued talking about The Walkabout and Ben's use of the tool. "Ben is the master of inspection. I saw him on our floor and watched him in our warehouse on his Walkabouts. He picks things up, shakes them, looks at them, flips them over, and touches them. He asks questions like, 'How's that new material working,' or 'Is that barcode system working well?' He asks questions to better understand our perspective of the work we're doing and is genuinely looking for answers."

Sophia probed for more, "Did he have a set path he took every day? Did he alternate his path to make sure he covered everything?"

"Nope," replied Aubrey, "although he was intentional, it just looked like he was wandering around, checking stuff out."

"I am sorry, but that sounds like a huge waste of time," Sophia looked perplexed.

"You might think so," Aubrey said. "But it is the furthest thing from it. Ben says people only respect what you inspect. And boy, is that the truth. Before Ben walked around, no one did. Our previous management would be in their offices all day, staring at their computer screens. When we did see them, we all were on our best behavior because we assumed they were coming to either yell at someone or worse. 'What are they doing here?' was mumbled under the breath of just about everyone every time we saw them."

Aubrey continued, "Seeing upper management on our floor was usually a sign of bad news. If they went to the warehouse, you knew heads were about to roll. Ben was different. The first couple days, it was weird. I admit seeing him just wandering about the place, asking questions and looking at stuff was odd. The managers on my floor were super nervous. The poor warehouse manager looked like he would pass out every time he saw Ben out on the floor. It just felt like he was out of place, and they didn't like it. However, the more time he spent out with us, the less worried we became. We were proud of the fact that the owner of the business was walking around inspecting things. He was genuinely interested in the work we did. He was curious and, over time, we became more curious, too. We looked forward to his walks. Many times, Ben would ask a question that would lead you to really think through your processes and improve them. We were excited to show off something we were really proud of or tell him about something that was working well. Ben only spent a few minutes a couple of times each day, but his presence lingered.

Aubrey looked as if she was reminiscing again. "We didn't just operate on our best behavior when Ben was there. We did it all the time. Before, we had no idea if management cared or even knew we existed, and that was never the case with Ben. We knew we were part of the team, and the CEO spent time each day just checking in on us. As Ben built out his executive team, those leaders all started walking as well. They were all connected to the front of the business where the action happened. It was great! Ben also made sure every manager had a number of critical tools and was using them every day. That way, all of the leadership in was on the same page. Ben called this 'common language.'"

"What would be an example of the common language?" Sophia asked.

"Well, all of the things we have been talking about." Aubrey shook her head in acknowledgement. "You probably noticed that Ben, Adam, and I all use similar terms. The Walkabout, The Adjust, Accountability, Huddles are all part of our common language. When I say 'Adjust', you know exactly what I mean, right?"

Sophia was excited to know the answer. "Of course! It is the four-step process to getting someone back on track."

"Exactly! And The Huddle?" Aubrey questioned.

Sophia sat up in her chair and repeated the answer like a fifth-grade spelling bee winner. "That is the stand-up meeting you run at the beginning or end of each shift."

"See," Aubrey replied, "we are all speaking the same language. Now, Adam runs his huddles a little differently than me because our businesses are different."

"What do you do differently in The Huddles?" Sophia asked.

"First, I run mine just once daily at the start of the day. Also, because the nature of work differs from the pace of a restaurant, the conversation is different.

"It's the same format, but I ask three questions:

1. What did you accomplish yesterday?
2. What will you accomplish today?
3. What is the barrier that will stop you from hitting that goal?

"I see," Sophia replied. "You modified the questions to fit your business needs."

"Exactly," acknowledged Aubrey. "Our agency is project-based. People depend on each other to deliver elements of a project. Many times, the bottlenecks are between the people in different departments. Using a model where people talk about what they have accomplished is good for us. It keeps everyone on point and on time. This also shows anyone that works here that we expect success. We don't only look at the long term, but we're interested in today. We expect every employee to contribute something meaningful every day."

Aubrey made a point to be deliberate, "We all use the same common language, but you could say there are different accents or dialects."

"That makes sense. It's like people from different parts of the country all speak English but, it sounds a little different based on where you're from." Sophia felt like she was really on to this new, common language.

"You got it!" Aubrey acknowledged. "A big part of our common language is the belief in an invisible force of Accountability. In this case, invisible doesn't mean you can't see it. The Huddle is the manifestation of the unseen. The force is at work, and you see it play out in The Huddle. Every morning, I need to be prepared and on my game. I tell the team what I accomplished yesterday. I commit myself to the team and the project I'm working on that day. And, I expose anything that might stop me. Something as simple as The Huddle is a very powerful tool.

"I love this idea of a common language!" Sophia exclaimed. "At The Diner, I would probably follow a model similar to Adam's, but it is good to know it is flexible based upon the demands of the business."

Aubrey shook her head in agreement as she said, "The key is doing it every day. It should be brief, fun and impactful. We have a silly tradition where the person speaking has to hold a stuffed bear. We throw the bear around to the next person whose turn it is to talk. It's a fun little thing that keeps it interesting. The bear has become something of a mascot. He celebrates birthdays and anniversaries, and someone even made costumes for every season you can imagine."

"That's great. It keeps it fun, and I guess you have to pay attention with a bear flying around," Sophia chuckled.

"Oh, yes," Aubrey nodded in an abbreviated fashion. "Drop that bear, and everyone will give you a hard time."

"That makes sense, Aubrey. Where do I start with all of this? Should I spend more time with Ben?"

"Sounds like you have already started. You said you have been using The Adjust, right, Sophia?"

"I only used it once. I like the idea of The Huddle, but I want to make sure I do it right before I start."

"Do it!" Aubrey said with such authority that it startled Sophia a bit. Aubrey continued, "Start the next day you are back at work. It doesn't have to be perfect. You need to get started. Gather your people together, and just start. Follow the script. Just ask them what they are proud of and what they think they can improve. It's easy to start."

Sophia shook her head and vocalized her concern. "The problem is, we are always taking care of customers. How can I get my team together when we have tables to attend? I just don't know how to make this work at The Diner."

"Ask Ben his ideas, but I would bet he will tell you that you either need to do it before or after the shift. You might consider mini-Huddles as part of your Walkabout. Just gather a few people from a department during a lull and do The Huddle."

"Thanks, Aubrey. It feels like there is so much to do. We are very far behind on systems or having processes. We really don't have any form of accountability. I have my work cut out for me."

"Sophia, you have to remember where you came from. Every day, every improvement, every Huddle, Adjust, and Walkabout you do is building the system. Every tool takes you one step farther away from chaos and a step closer to order."

"I guess so." Sophia shook her head feeling like she was shaking off some old belief. "What is the old saying? 'A journey of 1,000 miles begins with one step.' I guess I have taken my first step. Many more will follow. Well, I have to catch the train to get to class on time. Aubrey, thank you so much for your help today."

"Anytime! Maybe I'll see you at the office."

"Oh, yes. See you at the office," Sophia chuckled and smiled.

As Sophia sat down on the train, she removed her notebook from her backpack. She opened it to a fresh sheet of paper and began writing down all she had learned.

Chapter 5

Back to the diner

"Good morning, team." Sophia called out over the sound of clinking plates and calls of 'order up' coming from the kitchen.

"Good morning," came a choir of Anna, Miguel, and the others.

"How are things going?" Sophia inquired.

"Faster than ever," Miguel called out. "This cooktop is working great. But we have a new problem. Come back and see me when you have a second."

"Excellent, Miguel. Let me get a handle on everything, and I will come by in a bit."

"See you then," Miguel's voice trailed off as Sophia followed Anna out the door to a packed restaurant.

"Wow, Anna, you guys are slammed!" Sophia said with some excitement. "What needs to be done?"

"We got it, boss," Anna proudly exclaimed. "Everything is A-OK. Miguel and the guys in the kitchen are having a little glitch. Cooked food is coming out fast, but toast is another thing. That old toaster can't keep up. Now that plates are turning faster, the guys can't keep up with bagels, English muffins, and toast."

"I'll head back to see what I can do," Sophia said as she turned on her heels and headed to the kitchen.

"Miguel, what's up?"

"It's what ain't up is the problem," Miguel said if holding back to deliver a punchline. "Toast."

"So, I heard," acknowledged Sophia. "Anna said you guys had fallen behind on toasting bread and muffins?"

Miguel spoke faster than usual. "Yes, and no. I mean, we are still doing them at the same speed we did before. But, because the cooktop now works, we are faster on pushing plates out, which means toast lags behind the other food."

"I see. So, the barrier is a toaster?" Sophia asked. "If I get you a new toaster today, that should put out that fire … I mean solve that problem, right?"

"Yes, ma'am. Another toaster would double our capacity."

"Ok, Miguel. I'll call Rich."

Miguel interrupted Sophia's thoughts on the next step. "Before you do that, you might want to consider a conveyor toaster. I had one at my last job. It was great. You just laid in the bread or bagel, and the machine did the rest. It's much better than a toaster. "

"That makes sense, Miguel. I'll mention it to Rich. Anything else happening I should know about? Any other items you or the team has seen that would speed things up or make it easier?"

"Haven't thought much about it. Let me check with the guys."

"Sounds good," Sophia said as she headed toward the office to place a call.

·····••●●●••·····

"Hi, Rich. Its Sophia."

"What's up, Sophia?

"I wanted to talk to you about possibly getting a commercial conveyor toaster for the kitchen. Miguel and the team said that they are falling behind getting toast out because they can only do a few slices at a time. It is ok to buy one?"

"No!" Rich chirped back. "I am not spending any more money because Miguel is being lazy. Tell him to get off his ass and step up the pace. That toaster worked fine for years. We don't need some big expensive commercial do-hickey. Anything else?"

"Umm, well, ahh, no, I guess," Sophia stuttered, not knowing how to reply.

"OK, Sophia. Gotta run."

Sophia hung up the phone. "Well, that stinks. Rich just shut me down. He didn't want to hear why or how it would improve things. He just blamed us for being lazy. Doesn't he understand that things here are picking up? Our receipts are up. Our tables are turning faster. This is a bottleneck that limits our growth. What a jerk."

As Sophia pushed her chair back, she thought a moment about the items she wrote in her notebook. I want to develop people. I want to remove barriers. I want to provide resources. However, Rich is standing in the way.

"If Rich truly understood that, he would jump at the chance to help."

Sophia headed back out to the front hoping to catch Ben in between meetings. As she rounded the corner, she nearly ran head first into Ben.

Ben reacted to this near collusion like a man on a mission. "Sophia, I was coming to find you. I heard things went well with Adam, and I heard you met with Aubrey."

"Oh, Ben, yes, it was wonderful. I have a good feel now for the system. I learned all about The Adjust, The Huddle, The Walkabout, but … well, I am stuck."

"Stuck?" Ben inquired. "Well let's go to your office and talk about it."

"Oh, Ben, let's!"

Sophia opened the door to the little office, and Ben plopped down in the corner chair and immediately asked, "OK, what's going on?"

"Well, Ben, I started walking around a little, just listening, and Miguel showed me that half the cooktop didn't work. I jumped on it and worked with Rich. We got it fixed, and now look at this place. It's hopping."

"Good food doesn't take time, does it?" Ben said with a chuckle intentionally trying to recall Sophia to the conversation with Adam.

Sophia replied with an authority that Ben was unaware resided in Sophia's 5′ 4″ frame, "No, it does not!"

Sophia continued, "However, that decrease in cooking time has caused another problem. Our old, four-slice toaster isn't cutting it. The toast is coming out well after the food is ready."

"So, you need to remove a barrier and provide a resource?" Ben asked, already knowing the answer.

"Yes, but Rich shut me down," Sophia said in a forlorn tone.

"That's odd. Did Adam or Aubrey talk to you about awareness and outcomes?" Ben asked.

"Yes, so I called Rich and made him aware that toast was coming out slow. I told him we needed a commercial conveyor."

"How did you frame the conversation?" Ben asked.

"Frame? I called him and told him we needed it," Sophia said as if her expectation was far higher than her reality.

"Why did you need it?" Ben inquired.

"Simple, Ben. Things here are so much busier than before. Receipts are up, table turn times are down, and our deposits the last week are 30% more than ever before. The only way we can keep this up and grow more is to solve the problem of toast leaving the kitchen after the meal is served. The toast delay causes us to have to apologize to the customer, and it creates a little fire every time we serve a dish. Servers are rushing around to check on toast or bagels, and then rushing those back to the tables to apologize again. It's a vicious cycle."

"It sure is," Ben replied. "And you explained this to Rich with all this detail?"

"Well, no. I told him we needed another toaster."

Ben looked directly into Sophia's eyes as if to make a point, "But you missed telling him why."

"I guess I did. What do I do now?"

"Got your notebook?" Ben pointed to Sophia's notebook on the desk in front of her.

"Right here!" Sophia reached for her notebook and opened it to a fresh page.

"OK, Sophia. Let's make your case using awareness as our tool. First and foremost, anytime you need to remove a barrier or provide resources, and you need external help from someone else (someone who is senior to you, another department, or even another manager), always use these four steps."

"First, Sophia you need to give Rich awareness to the issue. Write down the word 'Awareness' in your notebook."

As Ben continued, Sophia began jotting in her notebook, recording the words and steps Ben was saying.

Awareness

- *Make the other party aware of the need or reasons:*

  - *Rich have you seen the deposits this last week?*
  - *Sales are up by XX%, and table turn times are down.*
  - *A fully working cooktop has sped up the time it takes to cook orders.*
  - *I have been working hard with the team to find new ways to make the process smoother and keep people accountable.*

- *Explain the benefits of the investment:*

  - *Sales are up with just the cooktop investment. This has caused another issue to show up. Now we need to invest in a faster toaster to keep up with the orders and give us a greater capacity to do even more.*
  - *A conveyor toaster will eliminate cooks standing around waiting for the bread to toast, then having to remove it and reload the toaster.*
  - *Our employees are hourly, so every minute wasted is a minute you paid for. Each minute standing around is a minute they could have been adding value somewhere else.*

- *Provide the data needed to make and support the decision:*

  - *Rich the new conveyor toaster costs $450 dollars.*
  - *It can be installed Tuesday*

- *Close with the expectation of success:*

  - *I am going get that ordered today. Does this sound good to you?*

"Oh, I get it!" Sophia exclaimed. "How could he say no to that?"

"He can't, or more likely, he won't." Ben continued, "When you called Rich before, you were asking him to spend money because it made things more convenient. This time, you are explaining the benefits to him, to the business, and your customers. You are providing him awareness to the outcomes. Rich can now see, or at least imagine, what things look like with this new toaster. Instead of it being another expense, it is now an investment in the future. A new toaster becomes a cost-cutting, profit-generating investment."

Ben concluded with, "I think you need to call Rich back right now. I am heading up to my other office for a meeting. Come find me after you make the call."

Sophia took out her notebook and jotted down a summary.

How to make the case for needed resources.

Anytime you need to remove a barrier or provide resources and you need external help from someone else (someone senior to you, another department or even another manager), always use these four steps.

1. *Provide awareness into the reasons*
2. *Explain the benefits of the investment*
3. *Provide the data/context needed to make and support the decision.*
4. *Close with the expectation of success.*

Chapter 6

Sophia, the Manager

"Ben, I have great news. The new toaster is ordered and will be here next week," Sophia said beaming with pride. "But get this. After I explained the reasons, Rich asked me to look into a milkshake mixer and get one installed if I felt it was the right decision." Sophia over emphasized the word "I" with pride. "It seems that years ago, The Diner offered milkshakes during the lunch rush, and they were very profitable. The hitch was they took time. After a while, the wait staff stopped offering them because they were a pain to make. I told Rich, 'Maybe one of those new machines would make it easier to put those back on the menu.' He said to get one if I thought it makes sense.

"I am excited! This feels like progress. We're moving farther from chaos and closer to order!"

"Well you should be excited," replied Ben. "It is progress. Rich was just exposed to Sophia, The Manager!"

"I know. It feels great!" Sophia bounced on her heels as she spoke. "I guess now that things are running more smoothly, Rich will expect me to do some of the other things he mentioned around marketing, hiring, and scheduling. I am stoked, but I'm also really nervous about it. Do you have any tools for that, Ben?"

"You know it! But first, tell me a little about what you learned from Adam and Aubrey."

Sophia opened her notebook and turned the page to Ben.

"Here is what I have so far."

Sophia turned around her notebook so Ben could see her notes on the system and the tools she had discovered.

"Sophia, this is a great start," Ben replied in a very serious tone. "Let me give you a little more to think about and offer you a new tool for your toolbox. First, when it comes to The Adjust, you can add the words 'hear' and 'understand' to the first step. Sometimes you witness something yourself. Other times, you might hear about a behavior that needs to change. At still other times, you might believe something is happening. Pick whichever one applies best. I see, I hear, I believe. Stay away from using, 'I feel' or 'I think' because I have found that people tend to argue more readily with thoughts and feelings."

"Second," Ben continued, "The Adjust is a great tool, but it is a tool of correction. It is intended to correct an undesired behavior to a desired behavior. A new tool for you, The Keep it Up, is a version of The Adjust that reinforces desired behaviors that you want to see continued or more of. You can, and should, use The Keep it Up every day as often as possible.

"The Keep it Up is similar:

1. I see, I hear, I understand … (be specific about the good actions or behaviors you want to see more of)
2. The benefits of that action are … (point out things that benefit customers, coworkers, the manager, or the business, in general).
3. Thank you, I really appreciate you … (be genuine in your acknowledgement)
4. I look forward to seeing more of (be specific again about the desired action or behavior) Keep it Up

Ben role played an imaginary conversation so Sophia would understand how the tool worked. "Justin, I heard from one of our customers you really went above and beyond while dealing with her child's allergies when she came by for lunch on Tuesday. That kind of attention is critical to our success. This is how we make regular customers. Thank you for taking the time to understand her situation. You did a great job. Keep it up."

Ben continued narrating the impact of the role play he just went over. "A simple conversation like this that takes just twenty seconds can go a long way. It doesn't have to be formal. The Keep it Up is a great way to give awareness to your people of the good things they do. The intention is to engage your team to create a better experience for everyone. A simple 'great work' is nice. But you have probably learned by now, knowing that we want to be clear with people, it is always best to iterate what specific action they took, when, and with whom. Keep in mind that The Keep it Up is generally addressed to an individual. You could use The Keep it Up on the team, but you need to make sure that it is as specific in terms of actions and behaviors as the individual Keep it Up."

"Wow! That is impactful, Ben. I have to say, I have never had a manager who went out of their way to praise me for the specific good things I was doing."

"It's the small stuff that adds up over time," Ben replied. "In this example, Justin just did what Justin should always do. But by praising him about the specific part of his action that he did, we reinforce the importance of the activity. Making Justin proud of what he does contributes to Justin showing up every day. Justin will probably stay with the company longer because of it. My experience is to do three Keep it Ups to every one Adjust. Although I rarely count, I just look for opportunities to use the Keep it Up more often than The Adjust. If my people only ever hear from me when I am adjusting behaviors, they will come to associate me with just corrective feedback. However, if I offer them praise and purpose along the way, they are more likely to accept the occasional correction and modify behavior."

"OK, so it looks like I need to write down a new tool." Sophia whipped out her notebook from her front apron pocket.

"You sure do," Ben replied. "The Keep it Up."

Sophia wrote each step in the book as Ben reminded her that The Keep it Up is not so much about doing it perfectly every time as it is about doing it often.

Ben added, "When I first start working with a manager, I would have them create a Keep it Up goal every day. This way, they are actively looking for good behavior, not just undesired behaviors."

"Santa Claus again!" Sophia exclaimed. "'He knows if you've been bad or good!'"

"Precisely, Sophia. You don't want your main communication with your people to always be a correction. If that is the case, when you do your Walkabout or move to a Position to Notice, people will be on edge thinking you are looking for compliance with the system or are quick to correct mistakes."

Sophia asked, "Ben what is the difference in Position to Notice and Walkabout?"

Ben replied, "Sophia, for the most part they are very similar. The Walkabout is more for managers that are not located where the work is happening and physically need to walk to that location. The Position to Notice is for managers that are working shoulder to shoulder with employees and need the reminder to remove themselves from the work so that they can manage people. Both techniques are deliberate and require the managers to physically move to the area or step back from doing the work. Make sense?"

Sophia nodded and Ben continued.

"Do you have time for another story?" Ben asked, wondering if Sophia needed to run.

"Of course, Ben, I have time!"

Ben proceeded to tell the story, "Years ago, when I worked in manufacturing, we had consultants come in to do time studies to see how long different processes took. Time studies would allow us to determine the cost of doing things and help us consider whether we should invest in automation or new machinery.

"The consultants gave us a worksheet that showed each time for each activity they measured.

"In addition to the time measured, they also showed a second measured time. At the top of that column they had the letters, 'MP.'

"We inquired what the MP numbers were and why they were better than the timed numbers.

"We were then told that 'MP' stood for 'Manager Present', and that these times were the times when our managers were on the floor. These were the times measured when people noticed they were being timed.

"In essence, when a manager was out on the floor for any reason, the pace of production increased by over 40 percent!

"Just by having a manager present, the people worked harder and produced more.

"Now, we could say an increase in time came from workers knowing the manager was there and wanting to look busy. Ultimately, it showed us performance suffers in the absence of accountability.

"Even though accountability is an invisible force, it is manifested through the tools, and The Walkabout is one of those tools.

"From that day forward, the management team committed to Walkabouts and never looked back."

Sophia let it all soak in for a second, connecting the dots between the story and her own experiences at The Diner. "I can see that. If Rich is there, we are all inclined to be on our best behavior. We clean a little deeper and move a little faster. I could see how a manager's presence steps up the activities of any employee."

"Exactly, Sophia. Most employees' experience with front line management tends be more negative than positive. It is important to use The Keep it Up more frequently than The Adjust. I try to use The Keep it Up at least one time per week with each employee, either formally or informally."

"I should make a note of that." Sophia jotted in her notebook, "Use The Keep it Up weekly with every employee."

Ben continued, "When you were over at Aubrey's, what did you see?"

"Wow, that place is amazing," Sophia said in an almost dreamy tone. "It is beautiful and bold."

Ben queried, "Did you see any of the 'perks', like the pool tables, free coffee bar, and snacks?"

"Yeah, that was really great!" Sophia exclaimed.

"I agree that sharing good stuff with your people is a good thing," Ben replied. "But a sugary latte, free candy, or a fun activity to do on a break doesn't say, 'thank you.' It says, 'We want you to think this place is fun.' However, work isn't always fun. It can be fun, but it can also be boring, monotonous, tedious, and stressful. It's like these companies put in a foosball table as an alternative to telling people how much they appreciate their work. I mean, what if you hate foosball?"

"I see. So, you aren't a fan of perks?" Sophia asked.

"On the contrary," Ben replied. "I think perks are OK, but only if you are already managing your people effectively. However, if you are using perks as some sort of motivation or veiled reward, they just don't work.

"Sophia, can I tell you another short story?" Ben went on before Sophia even had a chance to answer.

"One of my old clients prided themselves on having multiple employees who had been with them for more than ten years. People liked working there. The pay and benefits were good. They had a number of perks that employees enjoyed. All in all, the employees made a great team. The problem was they operated on a 'get stuff done' attitude where it was assumed everyone knew what needed to be done and would jump in where needed.

"We were working on a project trying to find the root cause of a continual stream of improperly billed invoices. We measured where their errors had originated. Once we identified where the issues were coming from, I sat down with the person that had caused the majority of errors and asked her about her performance. She told me she was good at her job and that in ten years there had been 'no complaints about her work'.

"I told her I wanted to present her with a spreadsheet showing all the errors in her department and wanted her to understand this was not about pointing fingers. The intention was to determine what we (as a management team) could improve to help reduce errors. She and I sat down and started through the sheet. She quickly realized that the majority of mistakes were coming from her individual data inputs. Some of these were minor errors or simple typos. Some were a misunderstanding of what was to be billed for the customers. Other errors were missed or added digits, like a $191.00 entry that was supposed to be $19.10.

"About one-third of the way through the sheet, she looked up at me, visibly shaken, and said, 'Why has no one ever told me?' I had no answer.

"Over the next two weeks, performance from this individual was almost error-free. She eagerly awaited the daily error summary to make improvements going forward.

"Unfortunately, at the end of those two weeks, and after ten years with the company, she quit. It was just too much for her. She could not get over how she had believed in all that time her performance was respectable and helpful to the team, then finding out she was the root cause of such a serious problem. She felt humiliated. But far worse to her was that, in ten years, no one had ever pointed that out to her, and that hurt.

"You see, no one was really managing her performance. It was never made clear to her. Not being clear with employees, and not telling them about their strengths and their weaknesses, is not fair to them. It's cruel. It limits them. It says you do not care about them.

"To loop it back to the beginning of the story, offering perks can be a nice gesture, but it doesn't make up for telling people how they are doing."

"Wow! That is sad," Sophia said with a bit of empathy. She could recognize how that must have felt. "She assumed she was doing well and, in the end, discovered she wasn't. That had to be embarrassing and hard to accept."

"It certainly was," Ben replied. "A lot of managers are not good at giving feedback. Most lack a system to do so. Funny, though, the root of managers not being well-versed at giving critical feedback mostly likely stems from childhood."

"This sounds like a psychology lesson or something Freud would say," Sophia said with a chuckle.

"Just a little psychology here, Sophia! Much of what the system is based upon is built upon understanding the psychology of people and human nature. An old saying you likely heard a hundred times growing up, 'If you don't have anything nice to say, then don't'—" Ben pointed to Sophia to finish the sentence.

"Say anything at all. My mother and grandmother said this to me all the time. I always thought it was good advice, no?"

"In most areas of life," Ben continued, "it is. However, that belief has made it hard for us, as managers, to give critical feedback at work. Instead, managers tend to avoid these opportunities because they told us saying negative things is bad. Rather than say something that might make someone feel uncomfortable, managers don't say anything at all. This is why it's so important to be clear to your employees."

"I see it now," Sophia replied. "I have avoided dozens of topics with friends because I didn't want to hurt their feelings or seem cruel."

"Effective feedback to improve is not cruel, is it?" Ben asked.

"I guess not. No, I know it isn't."

"So," Ben continued "tell people the truth, but do it using The Adjust and The Keep it Up as part of an ongoing process of critical and supportive feedback."

"That makes sense, Ben." Sophia glanced down at her watch and said, "Thanks, Ben. I guess I'd better get back to work."

"Get out there, Sophia. I see you making it happen. You are leading your team, making improvements, and that is good for everyone. It's good for you, this business, and future opportunities that await you! Keep up the great work."

"Thanks, Ben". Sophia smiled as she realized something, "Wait, did you just 'Keep it Up' me?"

Ben smirked.

"Thanks, Ben. Thanks again!"

Chapter 7

"Hi, Ben!"

"Hi, Sophia! How are you?"

"Ben, things are going well here at The Diner. We got the new equipment last week. I have started doing the scheduling myself, and Rich has asked me to start doing some marketing."

"Sounds great, Sophia. What does that mean, 'marketing'?"

"Marketing? Well, it means to advertise."

"What are you advertising?" Ben asked.

"Our food, our service, our location, I guess," Sophia replied.

"I see. And what is the outcome you expect from this marketing, Sophia?"

"Outcome? Um … more customers, I guess?"

"When do you want more customers, and what do you want them to buy?" Ben inquired.

"Ben, I don't know. I am not sure I'm that far along with what we will do and how."

"I see," Ben continued. "So, what exactly did Rich say?"

"He just said we need to do more marketing and that I should handle it."

Ben frowned, "Do you know what he meant by 'handle'?"

"Honestly, now that you say it, I don't." Sophia seemed frustrated by the continuous stream of questions. "No, I don't have any idea."

"Do you think Rich knows what he meant by 'handle'?" Ben probed.

"What is this, twenty questions, Ben? I hadn't thought of it. Honestly, he passed it off to me without much instruction or thought."

"That is my point, Sophia. Have you got your notebook?"

"Of course, Ben." Sophia settled in a seat at the bar next to Ben and got her notebook and pen ready.

Once settled, Ben spoke, "Write this down. It's another tool."

This Tool is called The ClariD's.

"C... L.... A.... R... I... D... S," Ben spelled it out and then continued, "When using The ClariD's, all requests must include the following four areas.

- It should include a Delegated accountable party.
- It should include a clearly Defined expected outcome.
- There needs to be a specific Deadline for completion.
- The most important part is that it must include regular status upDates on the progress.

"Anytime managers give or receive a request or project, like this marketing one, we have to answer a few questions. If unasked and unanswered, this will result in a lack of clarity. And to be unclear is ..." Ben pointed to Sophia.

"To be unkind, Ben. Adam told me."

Ben continued, "Clarity in requests is essential to success. If we fail to be clear about what we want from who, and when, we can do little more than hope to get what we want. You likely have heard the saying, 'If you want something done right, do it yourself.' If clear instruction had been given, you might not have had to do it yourself. Many times things fail, not for lack of effort, but for lack of clarity.

"The ClariD's is the tool for giving and receiving instruction. Let's talk about the conversation with Rich. Who is the accountable party for marketing?" Ben asked Sophia.

"Me," Sophia said with authority.

"Are you sure?" Ben probed, "Does Rich have a designer or a web person? Are you accountable for managing all of them as well? Is all instruction coming from you or him? With Rich and you, it's easier because it is just the two of you. But, imagine yourself in a corporate environment. Let's say you are on a call with ten people, and your boss says, 'I want you all to take charge of this project.' It is essential in that setting to clarify who, specifically, is the person in charge of the project. There has to be one central person to be held accountable."

"Should I just ask if there are any other resources we use for things like marketing?" Sophia asked.

"Absolutely," Ben replied. "Or, even ask about any marketing efforts The Diner is currently doing. You might find that Rich already does some things on his own. Are you accountable for those things as well?"

Ben asked, not expecting an answer, but instead to encourage Sophia to think about all the questions she might ask. "Next, we need to know not only what Rich wants, but also what outcome he expects. 'Handle the marketing' means nothing. As for clarity, get an accurate picture of Rich's expectations and the results he wants to achieve. Is it a 10 percent increase in tickets over the lunch hour? A 25 percent increase in milkshake sales? Don't accept the project as yours until you have answered what he expects as the outcome.

"Next," Ben continued, "When is the deadline for 'handling the marketing'? At what intervals will he, or you, measure success? Is this a one-time project focused around an event or season, or is this an ongoing effort that you must revisit at a specified interval? Finding out exactly when the results are expected is critical. And remember, ASAP is not a deadline. He needs to provide a specific date and time, for it to be considered a deadline. Friday the 30th at 5 p.m. is a deadline. 'Sometime next month' is not.

"Finally, set up a time to touch base, even if it's casual and just for a few minutes. Updating Rich on the status of the project makes sure he will get the outcome he wants. And it allows you both to discuss any barriers or bottlenecks that come up along the way.

"You need to make sure all four elements are a part of any delegation to you and from you. Remember, to be unclear is to be unkind."

"OK, I think I have it," Sophia replied and repeated back, "I need first to make sure that I am the one accountable for this project or if there are others that are working on parts as well. What if there are others doing parts? I do recall Rich once saying we have a webmaster."

Ben replied, "Then you either need to be accountable for the entire project and all its elements, or you need to know the outcome for the parts of which you are accountable. In business, not having 'the who' and 'the what' made clear creates a blame game. Employees working on the project will unwittingly create a big circle of finger pointing when things aren't done on time, completed on budget, or done correctly. Employees blame one another because no single person was accountable to make sure all the details worked together. If you find there are other people involved, ask him to assign you as the project lead. That way, you are the accountable party."

"Got it, Ben. Once I know if I'm accountable, the next thing I'll want to know is the desired outcome?"

"Precisely. What does success look like to Rich? If you know the deadline, it is easy to ask Rich to imagine precisely what things look like the day after the deadline. Let him daydream about what success looks and feels like. Say, for instance, the goal is to sell more milkshakes, 25 percent more to be specific. Then what will that look like on the deadline? How many dollars is that? Do you have latitude on flavors, or is this a chocolate and vanilla promotion only? Is there a price point he is comfortable with? Is he willing to discount or offer an incentive to reach that goal?" Sophia made copious notes while Ben was talking.

Sophia came back to reality to hear Ben's conclusion, "Being clear upfront creates an environment where success is not only attainable, but it's easy."

"So, I need to ask a lot of questions." Sophia spoke under her breath as she continued to write notes in her notebook.

"Yes," Ben replied, "To be frank, Rich might not have all the answers. But that is OK. You see, many times people delegate tasks as a form of punting."

"Like in football?" Sophia asked, puzzling how punting and business were related.

Ben continued, "Yes, they aren't sure what to do, so they dump the idea onto someone else with the hope that they will figure it out. Guess how often that happens?"

"I am guessing not too often," Sophia said while acknowledging the answer was right in front of her.

"Right. At the end of the project, they are content because they had no expectation to begin with, or worse, they dreamt up some secret expectation and assumed people understood it."

Sophia interjected, "What do you mean by a secret expectation?"

Ben replied, "A secret expectation is where you expect something in your mind, but you have never told the other person about it. For instance, you are the manager, and you always show up thirty minutes early for your shift because you like to be early. Does your showing up early mean you expect your team to show up early as well?"

"Of course not. That is just the routine I prefer," Sophia replied.

"Right," Ben continued, "It would surprise you how many times employees assume a manager expects them to show up early or stay late because that's what the manager does. In some companies, it is considered to be very inappropriate to leave before your manager or to show up for work later than management. In that environment, a secret expectation of long hours is in place, even though long hours are not a written job requirement. Therefore, it is essential to communicate exact expectations and requirements, so they know what is expected and what is not. If you don't do that, people start assuming and assuming—"

Sophia interrupted Ben as he had hoped she would. "Yes, I know. I know. Never assume."

"Precisely, that is the way you must manage people, Sophia. Manage with precision, clarity, and awareness."

"Ben, I can see why the update is important. Instead of waiting until the end, regular check-ins ensure that things are progressing. If problems occur, they have an opportunity to get resolved."

"You've got it now," Ben said hurriedly. "So, the next time Rich mentions marketing, do you have a plan?"

"Well, no, Ben," Sophia said with a sly smirk on her face. "I have a system to follow, but I think I better write out a plan."

"I agree," Ben replied. "Write down the questions you will ask to get the most out of the project expectations and timeline. Any time someone give you an assignment, make sure you have all four of the ClariD's to assure the project will run smoothly. In your world at The Diner, you might not use this tool as often as the others. Adam doesn't, but Aubrey uses it multiple times each day. Starting now is good practice for when you get greater responsibilities in your professional career."

"Thanks, Ben. So now I have five tools after I add in The Keep it Up and The ClariD's. What's next?"

"For now, Sophia, you have your work cut out for you. Every day you should be: running Huddles, intentionally walking around on your Walkabouts, and proactively looking for opportunities to use The Keep it Up to reinforce good actions from team members. You should be using The Adjust to get team members with undesirable behaviors back on track and you must use your ClariD's every time you delegate, or are delegated, a task."

"In addition, you also should have a fire map to pinpoint business 'fires' as they occur."

"That is a lot," Sophia acknowledged as she shook her head. "The tools seem like something I can do each day quite easily. Any other tools or tips I can use, Ben?"

"Although it seems easy, practice makes permanent. In time, with regular practice, these activities become second nature. Much like habits we have in our personal life, these tools become the 'Habits of Management'. Get out there, use them every day, hold yourself accountable, and I will hold you accountable as well."

"OK, Ben, you are right. Learning is one thing, doing is another."

"Sophia, I'll be out of town next week. How about if I see you when I get back to the office to see how you are doing?"

"You got it!"

Chapter 8
New Hire

Sophia was excited about her new hire. "So that about sums up the job duties and expectations. Lauren, your experience is impressive, and we would love to have you join our team as a server."

"Oh, that would be great," Lauren said as she happily acknowledged her new position. "When can I start?"

"Lauren, I could use your help tomorrow morning, bright and early."

"What time?" Lauren inquired.

"We do our morning huddle at 5:15 a.m. sharp. See you then, Lauren."

"Yes, see you then, Sophia."

Sophia turned back to her desk to add her first new hire to the schedule. The morning rush has extended into an all-day rush. The addition of milkshakes had not only increased the counter business, but takeout milkshakes for many local offices had become popular. Sophia was even preparing an online menu with the objective of adding Uber Eats delivery service by the end of the month.

As Sophia added Lauren to the schedule, it dawned on her that tomorrow morning after The Huddle, she would be doing precisely what Rich had done to her when she started. He had given her a thirty-minute tour, showed her how to enter and receive payment for tickets, handed her an apron, and threw her to the wolves.

"Sorry, that just won't cut it," Sophia said to herself.

"There has to be a better way of making sure Lauren gets adequately trained and understands the importance of the things we do. Otherwise, we risk shutting the door on accountability and sliding backward towards chaos. I need another body out front tomorrow, but I wonder if there is a better way to train Lauren.

"I wonder if Ben is here today?"

Sophia shot down the hallway on a mission to find Ben. She managed to catch Ben just as he was heading out the door.

"Ben, got a minute?"

"I sure do. How are things here, Sophia?"

"Good, Ben. The system is working well. Every day I remind myself of all the items I need to tick off my to-do list.

"I do my Huddles at the beginning and end of each shift. I do two walkabouts each day, asking questions,

112

observing, and inspecting things. I set myself a goal of one Keep it Up per week per employee. I keep a little running tab in my notebook each day." Sophia pulled out her notebook and showed Ben her checkbox system.

Walkabouts ☐☐☐
Keep it Up's ☐☐☐☐☐☐
Team Huddles ☐☐

"I figure everyone deserves to know the things they are doing well.

"I use my ClariD's and Adjust as needed."

"What is your favorite tool?" Ben asked.

"Walkabouts, for sure, are my favorite," Sophia continued. "The Huddles are great. They are quick and easy. They serve an essential part in letting everyone know that I am always here, always listening and always open to destroying barriers. I love The Keep it Up. It really keeps me focused on noticing desired behaviors and easily correcting undesired behaviors. Finding at least one positive thing to praise someone about each week really keeps me looking through the lens of all the good things we do and accomplish here. The few times I have had to use The Adjust, it didn't feel overwhelming. It doesn't really even feel like correction anymore. It feels more like … um …"

"Coaching?" Ben inquired.

"Yeah, coaching," Sophia said with a slow head nod. "It felt like I was in it to help them be better and not just better for my sake, but for theirs. It feels good to develop them into being more professional."

"Sometimes saying something corrective is the most helpful thing you can ever say," Ben replied.

"Wow, I hadn't thought of that, Ben. By making someone aware of their shortcomings, I am giving them the opportunity to be better. If I don't do that, maybe no one ever will. It just becomes a lost opportunity for growth."

"Exactly. Can I tell you a personal story?"

"Of course," Sophia replied. "Are you sure you have time. I saw you were just heading out."

Ben replied, "I have a few minutes. So, back when I was a young salesperson, I got a good job doing sales for a service-based company. I was outgoing, focused, and driven. I did quite well. I did so well that I got promoted to overseeing a territory and had six other reps I was accountable for managing.

"However, being promoted over them was not taken all that well by some members of the team. I struggled to get them to continue to sell at the level they had in the past, and it was self-evident they lacked respect for me in a management role.

"My boss was a great guy. I asked him for his advice. It stung a little, but this is what he said. 'Ben, you are a great guy. You are a good salesman, and you have the makings of a great manager. However, you don't dress the part. Take a look at your people. They are well-dressed. Their polo shirts are tucked in, they have nice, pressed khakis, nice shoes, and they all have a sports coat hanging in their office in case they need it.

'You are their boss now, and you dress a peg below them. Your shirt is untucked, you wear more comfortable shoes than they do, and I don't know if I have ever seen you with a jacket. If you want to earn their respect and improve your ability to manage them and the customers, upgrade your wardrobe.'"

"I'll admit, his feedback stung a bit. I never really paid much attention to my clothes. Polo shirt, khakis, and dress shoes were the dress code. I pushed the lower limits of it. Some of my team dressed far better than I did, but most certainly all of them dressed at least slightly better.

"I committed that day to improve. I decided to wear button-down shirts. I upgraded to a dressier pant and decided to buy good, higher-end dress shoes.

"The new wardrobe probably cost me a week's pay. However, the results were immediate. The team respected me more. They took me out to see customers more often, and they seemed proud to introduce me as their boss.

"I even bought a couple of suits and wore those when I went out with my team in the field to meet their customers.

"My boss noticed as well, and he promoted me again to oversee five additional territories.

"I look back now and realize my performance was secondary to my image. The advice my boss gave me was most valuable. It was uncomfortable for me, but I would imagine it might have been awkward for him. To truly get the most out of me, and for me to get the most out of my career, it needed to be said."

"Wow, I never thought about something like that, Ben. I think I would be too embarrassed to even say anything like that. Thankfully, your boss did."

Ben continued, "I can't imagine where I would be today without that advice. The point is, being clear and coaching doesn't mean telling them they are doing a good job. It also means telling them what they can do to improve. Can you imagine a sports coach that wouldn't tell a player how to improve, but instead only told them the good stuff?"

"Of course not! How could they ever get better without knowing what needed to be improved?" Sophia said, almost disgusted at the thought of a coach not improving their players.

"Right," Ben continued. "So make it a point in business to do the same. The Adjust is an excellent tool for correcting undesirable behavior. It is a great training and coaching tool that can help your team members be better. Best of all, when The Adjust is part of a loop of continuous feedback including The Keep it Up, people won't take it the wrong way. They will acknowledge the corrective coaching as part of a series of comments you have provided them as a pathway to improvement.

"I am sorry, Sophia. I started telling you a story when I think you came over here to ask me something. Did you have a question for me?"

"Oh, yes, Ben. I recently hired a new server to help out. Her name is Lauren, and she starts tomorrow. After thinking it over, I am concerned that I will fall into the old pattern of giving her the tour, showing her how to use the POS system, and then throwing her into the mix. I don't that is fair to her. What are your thoughts?"

Ben nodded his head in agreement. "Throwing someone into a process is not only a terrible idea for them, but it runs the risk of creating a deviation from the established process. Sophia, we have talked about the tools, and you have heard about the importance of processes, but do you have SOPs?"

"SOPs?" Sophia said reaching for her notebook.

Ben allowed Sophia a moment to get to a blank page before continuing. "Do you have Standard Operating Procedures? They are documented processes that everyone can see and follow."

Sophia's eyes lit up. "Oh, do you mean like the ones Adam had in the kitchen and at the wait station at Emanuel's? They were step-by-step pictures of what needed to be done. They reminded me of IKEA furniture instructions. They were simple to understand, step-by-step."

"Yes, those are SOPs," Ben acknowledged. "Does The Diner have any?"

"Not written down, Ben. We have them in our heads."

"And what if one of those heads is a no-show tomorrow? What then?" Ben inquired.

"I guess I hadn't thought about it. Oh no, I likely shouldn't have hired Lauren yet." Sophia said while turning pale.

"Not necessarily," Ben replied. "A new hire is an excellent time to start SOPs. See, the first days and weeks that a new hire is working, they ask a lot of questions, right?"

"They sure do!" Sophia bellowed, recalling past employees and mimicking their vocal patterns. "'How do you do this?'" she proclaimed in a deep, manly voice. "'Can you show me that again, Sophia?'" she said again, this time mimicking the voice of frail, older woman. "All the questions can drive me crazy."

"But they also ask an even more critical question than how things are done. They all ask a question that you should pay close attention to: 'why?' New employees are trying to understand the new processes, and they will ask both how and why. Why is essential because it tells you that the reason is not obvious. This could mean that you are blind to an inefficiency. For example, 'Why do we brew the coffee in the back of the kitchen? Why not brew it up here behind the counter?' Questions like that are generally answered with the old standby, 'That's just the way we do things around here.' They may even hear a reason that makes sense by itself but makes no sense from an efficiency perspective. 'There's no place to plug that coffee maker in out here, so we have to run back and forth.'"

"Wait, that's a barrier," Sophia eyes lit up and her new managerial sense tingled inside her.

"Exactly," said Ben. "It seems to make sense that there is no place to plug in the coffee maker, so it must stay in the back. That is unless you think about the extra cost of it being in the back, and you make the case that running a new outlet makes more sense."

"Like the conversation with Rich about the toaster?" Sophia interjected. "You always have to make a case for why it needs to happen."

"You got it, Sophia. The cost of moving an outlet is probably $100 dollars, but the cost of leaving it where it is might be $100 dollars a day. If you are open 360 days a year, that outlet's placement costs $3,600 a year in lost profits. That's $3,600, which might be invested in new equipment, raises, or upgrades. Smart managers are on the lookout for these things. They are continually asking why things are the way they are. The smartest manager finds these inefficiencies. They resolve inefficiencies, then determine how much those changes saved. And, they keep a running total.

Ben continued, "Think about a conversation with Rich where you want to upgrade something or add a new piece of equipment. With data, you can go back and remind him that the cooktop saved X dollars in labor and increased table turns by Y%."

"I love that. Instead of it being about spending money, it is about saving money!" Sophia exclaimed.

"And using the savings to save more," Ben added, nodding to Anna as she passed by and pushing his coffee cup towards her for a refill.

"Great idea, Ben."

"Back to your question about onboarding. Your new person is Lauren, right?" Ben inquired.

"Yes," Sophia said as she watched Anna pour a fresh cup of black coffee for Ben.

Ben continued, "Since the SOPs are not yet in place, explain to her that, as part of her onboarding, you will train her and she will document the process. This allows you to create the SOPs in real time. By documenting the process, it will encourage everyone to ask questions about the processes and start improving them even before you have them finished."

"How do I document this stuff?" Sophia asked, feeling perplexed with the daunting nature of the task.

Ben spoke assuring Sophia, "The easiest way is with a process diagram. That can be as simple as bubbles on a paper and lines connecting each step. It could also be post-it notes on a wall in the office showing each step of a process."

"Can you show me?" Sophia asked, hoping that Ben would.

Sophia slid her notebook across the table to Ben.

"Sure." Ben began by drawing a single small circle on the top of the blank page. "What is the first step in your process for a server?"

"The first step is to take the customer's order," Sophia replied.

Ben pushed back, "That is part of the process, but is that the first step?"

"Oh, right, Ben. It would be taking the drink order."

Ben pushed back again, "Think even farther back than that. What is the first interaction the customer has with The Diner?"

"I guess when they walk through the door?" Sophia's answer was more of a question now as she looked to Ben for confirmation.

Ben shook his head and said, "It probably starts even earlier than that with their stomach grumbling. But for this purpose, let's start with the door. Imagine for a moment you had never been here before. What would it be like to walk into the sights, sounds, and smells of a busy—"

Sophia interjected with a side note of her experience, "Sorry to interrupt, but this happened to me the day we met at Emanuel's. I walked in like a deer in headlights."

"And, what got you out of that feeling of confusion?" Ben asked.

"The hostess!" Sophia said while thinking back to that experience. "She immediately greeted me and made me feel welcome."

"And here at The Diner, who is accountable to do just that?" Ben inquired.

Sophia thought for a moment. "Right now, it is no one. We only have a sign that tells customers to seat themselves."

"That is fine if that's the way you want to run the business, and the customer doesn't mind." Ben nodded his head as if to agree with the process. "Have you ever had customers not seat themselves?"

Sophia replied, "Sure, all the time. They stand there waiting as if they expect us to seat them."

"What happens then, Sophia?" Ben inquired.

"One of us hollers over to tell them to seat themselves."

Ben looked unamused as he continued, "And who is at fault for them standing there?"

"Well, they are, of course. Our inside joke is to say they are 'TDTRTS'," Sophia said with a girlish giggle.

"TDTRTS?" Ben asked.

"Too dumb to read the sign. TDTRTS," Sophia laughed out loud as if telling Ben a funny joke.

Ben either refused to laugh or didn't think the joke was funny as he asked, "May I coach you a bit?"

"Why not!" exclaimed Sophia, feeling a bit knocked down that Ben didn't acknowledge her sense of humor.

Ben continued, "In Japan, the first rule of management is that humans do not make mistakes. If a mistake has occurred, it results from a system or process that is inefficient or ineffective. Thus, management is responsible."

"Wait, so you are saying people not reading the sign is partially my fault?" Sophia gazed at Ben in a bit of shock.

Ben piped in, "Oh, no, Sophia. I am not saying it is **partially** your fault." Ben let Sophia recover a bit then hit really dropped the bomb on her. "Sophia, it is 100 percent your fault. These are your customers, and if the system in place isn't working for them, it is your fault."

"Owww!" Sophia reeled back reacting as if a school yard bully just caught her with a left hook. "That hurts, Ben." Sophia continued acknowledging her revelation, "People not seeing the sign means the sign isn't big enough, it isn't visible enough, or the sign makes no sense."

Sophia looked like she had been punched in the stomach as Ben continued, "It's the same experience that happened to you at Emanuel's. While you were observing everything, your mind was racing. All that was happening around you overwhelmed you for a moment. It took the hostess to draw you out of it. It is same thing here."

"I see now. So, what do you suggest? Do I need to make a bigger sign?" Sophia asked as if she had a solution.

"Probably not," Ben replied. "Is a big sign the experience you want? Also, will some customers still ignore it? Think about your experience at Adam's place. What drew you out of your temporary coma while you were overwhelmed upon entering?"

Sophia blurted out, "The hostess did. Are you suggesting we have a hostess?"

Ben was quick to reply, "No, not if that isn't who The Diner wants to be. Instead, what if you made a point of welcoming each guest upon their arrival and quickly pointing out they can choose any seat they like."

"Everyone doing this, or …?" Sophia asked as she puzzled on how this would even work.

Ben continued, "Make it a proximity rule. Anyone within fifteen feet of the door says 'hello', welcomes the customer, and tells them to have a seat."

Sophia pondered for a moment. "I could see that working for the most part. What if no one is there?"

"Then you need to think about how the whole thing works," Ben replied. "Play it out in your mind. Maybe the person behind the counter is the default. Do you have a bell that rings when people enter? It would help if you role-played it. Ask your people. Start somewhere, and then improve upon that. A good process is not about being perfect out of the gate. It is just about being better than yesterday. You should write that down, Sophia."

Sophia picked up her pen and reached out to the notebook with one small circle on the page. Once it sat in front of her, she picked up her pen and made a note.

"Process is not about being perfect. It is about being better than yesterday."

Ben went on as Sophia was writing. "Too many businesses think their processes must be perfect before they can implement improvements. Managers sometimes fear that rolling something new out, then having to alter it will make management look weak or inadequate. To the contrary, the best leaders know that everything is a work in progress and to embrace suggestions, improvements, and ideas and integrate them into their system to make things better every day."

"I like that," Sophia said as she repeated it. "Better every day. Sometimes, I feel like I am failing at leading, but if I ask myself what we are doing better today than yesterday, that gives me hope. I have hope that things are improving. There are fewer fires, fewer challenges, more accountability, and less chaos."

"Now you have it, Sophia," Ben said with some pride. "And you, my friend, just led yourself to the final tool. This is the final tool for now, at least."

"What is the final tool?" Sophia said excitedly.

Chapter 9

"1% better every day."

"One percent better every day," Ben said as he took a long drink of his coffee, allowing Sophia a moment to jot it down.

Ben sat down his cup and motioned to Anna that he was done by holding out his hand and pushing it away over his cup like a blackjack player who is content with the hand he holds. Ben continued, "Every day your challenge should be to improve something by one percent. Share that goal with your people and have them participate as well. Constantly ask yourself, 'Is there a way to make this order one percent faster, one percent more appealing with one percent less waste? Can I satisfy the customer by one percent more today than yesterday?'"

Ben said the next piece slowly, intentionally, enunciating each word. "Focus on continuous, incremental improvement."

"OK, I like that," Sophia said as she again went back to her notebook to write down what Ben was saying. As she wrote the last letter, she looked up at Ben and inquired, "But Ben, I need big ideas. Improving by just one percent seems silly and pointless. One percent is not much. It seems too easy."

"That is where you are wrong, Sophia. One percent improvement each day equals 3,800 percent improvement annually. If you make something one percent better today, then again improve tomorrow, and the next, and next day, over and over, the system or process is eventually exponentially better.

"As you said, one percent is easy. One percent is without excuses. Anyone can do one percent." Ben continued, "If Rich asked you to improve this place by 1,000 percent this year, what would you think?"

"He's crazy," she said, "is what I would think."

"Yet, think about it Sophia. One percent each day gets you far more than 1,000 percent."

"I see. Incremental improvement equals exponential results!" Sophia exclaimed.

Ben looked at Sophia, "Hand me back that notebook. I need to write that down."

"Ha! The master becomes the student!" Sophia said with excitement realizing that she got it, and that her understanding was even new to Ben.

"Absolutely," Ben said. "This is why I do what I do. This is also why The Walkabout is so essential. The ideas are out there. The improvements that take you from loss to profit are locked up in someone's head. We just rarely ask for them."

Ben continued, "I get to see and hear diverse perspectives from all sorts of people at all levels on their management journey. From CEOs to front-line managers, many of their problems are the same. For the most part, they are caused by a lack of awareness and fundamental tools."

"CEOs struggle with these things?" Sophia inquired. "I mean, come on. Those big corporations run like well-oiled machines."

"Oh, Sophia, if you only knew. When companies get bigger, problems get bigger and more frequent. Often, those leaders tend to forget the fundamentals that got them there. They become so focused on avoiding big risks that they cannot see the small risks in front of them. You, Adam, and Aubrey all share a common language even though you don't work in the same company. That common language might have distinct accents or dialects based on the business, but if we brought up a conversation about the Walkabout, ClariD's, The Adjust, The Keep it Up, Huddles or The One Percent, any one of you can immediately engage in a conversation about how you use them and the results you are seeing.

Ben slowed his pace as if acknowledging that, no matter the size, all companies struggle with the same basic things. "Big companies might seem like they have it all together, but common language, common tools, and good management practices are not always in place. In some cases, there are more assumptions in big business than in small."

Sophia piped in, "And Assumptions make an ASS out of ..."

"... U and Me!" they both chimed together in unison.

"So back to the process," he said. "Write it down as I say it."

Sophia clutched her pencil and began to write as Ben spoke.

"Step one is to greet the customer and ask them to be seated." He pointed forcefully at Sophia's notepad. "Who is accountable for that action?" he asked.

"Anyone within fifteen feet from the door, or the counter person by default," Sophia replied.

"Excellent. And when should they greet them, Sophia?"

"Well," Sophia responded, "it depends on who is there and what they are doing at that time."

"It might," Ben interjected. "But set a rule, a standard, a guideline that we can all abide by—say ten seconds. 'Within ten seconds of the time a customer enters, they are welcomed.'"

"I could see that. I mean, sometimes we might have a couple of people greeting them at the same time. Is that OK, Ben?"

"Would that be a problem," he asked, "over-welcoming your guest?"

130

"No, it wouldn't. It would be nice, actually."

"Exactly," Ben replied.

"So, what do we have so far?" Ben asked.

"Step one is that all team members within fifteen feet of the door will greet each customer within ten seconds of the time they enter the door, with the counter person always welcoming them as well."

"What is Step two?" Ben pointed to Sophia to continue.

"Take their drink order?" Sophia wasn't terribly confident with her answer.

"Is it?" Ben asked in that tone Sophia had become accustom to. She knew Ben is was really asking her to try again. "Think about it."

Sophia pondered for a moment and then took a shot at answering the question. "I guess if we really want to get granular, it would be to welcome them again at the table."

"OK," Ben said, "Think about how you would greet me."

"Hmm," Sophia deliberated for a moment. She was not sure if she was to answer.

After a long awkward pause, Ben spoke up, "Let's role play this. Talk to me as if you were just greeting me at the table."

"Um, OK, I guess ... Good morning, can I get you started this morning with a coffee or tea?"

"Yes, please. I'll have a coffee," Ben replied.

"Would you like cream or sugar? Can I get you any water or juice?"

"No, thanks. Black is fine."

"We have a special this morning. It's biscuits and gravy with your choice of sides. I'll give you a moment while I get your coffee."

"Thank you."

"How'd that feel?" Ben inquired, knowing full well from Sophia's demeanor that she was wildly uncomfortable with what just happened.

"It was super weird, Ben. I didn't like it at all. It felt uncomfortable."

"Why?" Ben asked, "Don't you do that all day long, Sophia?"

"Well, yes. But playing at doing it didn't feel natural."

Ben let out a little chuckle. "That's OK. It doesn't have to at first. However, role-playing is one of the best things you can do with your team. Just make believe a customer is here and let them practice. Do you see how that could help Lauren? Give her a specific set of questions and make sure that she asks them in that order every time before you turn her loose. You should let her practice with you a few times."

"I could do that. To me, it's just second nature, and I assume …" Sophia stopped herself and smiled. "OK, I got it. I can't assume that she knows the routine. If I do, she might retrieve coffee and then discover that the customer wants cream or sugar. Or, she returns, and the customer asks about specials. They may need a few more moments to decide what they are having. By having a specific order and specific questions, it makes for a better customer experience."

"This creates fewer steps for yourself. Think about it. How many steps do you walk here each day at The Diner?" Ben probed, knowing the answer would be more than even he could imagine.

"Less now," Sophia replied. "As a server, I walked a ton. I wear a Fitbit to track my steps, and the difference between a day working and my day off is crazy. I used to get at least 15,000 steps per shift when I worked as a server. My phone would tell me that is 7.5 miles!"

"Your work was your workout?" Ben laughed.

"Yeah, I guess so, Ben. I got my steps in every day I worked."

Ben continued, "That might be an OK thing for your cardio health. If everyone is doing that, you are paying people to walk around. Each step costs something. Fifty steps here and there add up to miles and miles of walking, and when you are walking, customers are waiting."

"I hadn't thought of that. Walking is waiting," Sophia said while thinking back to how many days she left work with her feet aching and calves burning from all the rushing around.

"Creating a process that reduces the number of steps is vital. In other businesses, we say that repeating a step or having missed something is considered *rework*. We have to do more work on the order because we failed to do the job properly in the first place. Delivering a cup of coffee without having asked how they like it is rework. It causes you to have to return to the place where those ingredients are and then back again to the customer. Walking is waiting. While you are doing it, your customer is waiting, and all of the other customers are, too. Does that make sense, Sophia?"

"Yes, I can see why I want to make sure Lauren follows the processes we establish."

"Certainly," Ben said, "if you want to get the most out of the investment you are making in her."

Sophia piped in, questioning the whole idea of it all. "Doesn't that seem like we are exploiting her a bit? I mean, what does she get out of it? I see what Rich gets. He earns more profit, but what is in it for Lauren?"

"A lot more than you think," Ben replied. "Have you ever heard someone say they are stressed out at work or have too much on their plate?"

Sophia thought back to a career of over hearing customer conversations. "That is probably the thing I overhear the most."

Ben continued, "A good portion of that overworked feeling is the result of processes that are not streamlined, causing extra steps, exhaustion, fatigue, and stress. Training Lauren to do things the most efficient way is good for the business, but it is also good for Lauren and her customers. If Lauren turns tables over faster or is more attentive, will that help her?"

"Of course. The more efficient and proficient Lauren is, the more tickets and more tips she could earn," Sophia replied.

"Precisely, and Lauren walking less will cause her to be less frenzied when serving customers."

Sophia replied, "That is good, too. She'll have less stress and fewer steps."

Ben shook his head and pointed back at Sophia's notebook. "Step two is developing your scripts. Is there a way you might improve them by one percent?"

"Hmmm," Sophia pondered. "I need to think on that. Any ideas, Ben?"

Ben asked Sophia directly, "Do you know what percentage of your customers order coffee with their breakfast?"

"All of them?" replied Sophia.

"It can't be all, Sophia."

"No, Ben. I guess not, but certainly almost all order coffee."

"Sophia, you should find out. Check the receipts. If half or more of the customer's order coffee at their table, a process improvement might be to take it with you."

Sophia pondered that point for a moment to think about how that would work. Could wait staff carry a pot of coffee in one hand and mugs in the other?

Ben continued, "Or, how about setting the tables with coffee mugs instead of bringing them from the kitchen?"

"Hmm," Sophia reimagined the image in her head and muttered aloud while looking up at the ceiling. "I never thought of that. That might work well."

"Now is the time to do it, Sophia. Lauren is new. Teach her the correct way to do everything. Check your receipts today and make the change. Tell everyone at tomorrow's Huddle and put it into place. At the end-of-shift Huddle, ask how it went. Ask your team how they think the process could be improved. Make sure to tell people you are trying this for two weeks to see if it improves things.

"Because this is new and different, you might get some complaints from the servers for the first couple of days.

Know they will adapt, and they will feel part of the process. Be honest about whether it's working or not. Don't be afraid to say that didn't work."

Ben continued, "Too many managers are afraid to say their idea didn't work as planned. They aren't honest with themselves about what determined success or failure and would rather double down on a failed strategy than abandon the strategy and deal with the sunk costs."

"Sunk costs?" Sophia inquired.

"Sunk costs are considered money spent that can't be recovered," Ben replied. "Say, for instance, your new milkshake strategy failed, and no one was buying them. Because you spent money on the machine, you might be inclined to keep wasting time and money on trying to make it work. Even when no one wants to buy the product, many companies keep offering it, rather than admit they made a mistake. That is considered sunk costs. Be honest with yourself. Use data to help make decisions. If something isn't working, try modifying it to get it to work. In the end, always be willing to walk away from an idea that did not pan out as you'd expected."

"I see," Sophia said as if actually seeing it in her mind's eye.

Ben pointed back to the notebook, "Back to our steps; are you seeing how this works?"

Sophia snapped back to the notebook and the conversation, making some mental notes about trying the coffee process.

Ben continued, "Document each step, and make sure to think about it from multiple perspectives. Consider how this works for the customer, how it impacts other processes, how it benefits our team. You can role play the steps. If you are training on new processes, train with a new team member. If you are just creating a new process, think it through by yourself. Think through all the ways things could go right or wrong and accommodate those things. Remember, the process does not need to be perfect. It just needs to be better than before. Better doesn't mean radically different. One percent better is the goal. A sage woman once said to me, 'Incremental improvement equals exponential results.'"

"Hey, that's me! I said that!" Sophia said excitedly.

"It sure was, Sophia. That's a good line, and I am adopting it."

"Feel free to!" Sophia said with pride.

"You know what you need to do now, Sophia. Write out the steps for the things Lauren is accountable for. Train her on those steps. Tell her that you do things differently at The Diner. You are a team, and that means that once she learns the system, she will be able to contribute and improve it. I usually ask new employees to keep track of all of the times they ask why we do something the way we do. I also request that they share them with me each day. However, I also tell them that their job in the first few weeks is to learn the role. Learn how we do it first. Then, help us improve.

Ben continued, "Sometimes, asking people for ideas before they understand the whole process is a terrible idea. They don't yet completely understand how the business operates, so it isn't fair to you or them to burden them with thinking about how to make things better."

"I think have it, Ben. For now, just write the process on a piece of paper or post-its, and train her on that?"

"Yes. For now, that is enough. Make sure she sees the process and understands it *is* a process. Don't just tell her, show her. Give her a copy of it or leave it on the wall so she can refer to it. Use The Adjust and The Keep it Up every day for a while with Lauren. Praise her for the things she is doing well and Adjust her to things that need improvement. This will start her off on the right foot and set up a tremendous two-way relationship for as long as she works here."

"Love it," replied Sophia. "For now, keep The One Percent tool to myself?"

"For now, yes. However, it is not about hiding it. Just tell her to follow the process. Have her document her questions, and she will be able to work on improvements just like every other member of the team when she's ready. When you feel comfortable with it, you can start to introduce the one percent concept to your team."

"That would be great," Sophia replied.

Ben urged, "I suggest first rolling out The One Percent during your Walkabout. As you are walking around, ask people about the processes they follow, and challenge them to find a way to make a small improvement. You might be surprised. Remember, they are the experts at their work, and they might relish the chance to share their ideas. It is important really to emphasize The One Percent as a very small improvement. Ask them to think about their process from the most incremental perspective. Give them some examples to work with.

"They will likely have different perspectives, so I generally have employees think about their processes through four different lenses. I ask four basic questions and then have them ask themselves, as well. I use a little quip I made to remember them: automate, outsource, abbreviate, eliminate.

I always ask myself is there a way to automate this process? Is this something someone on our team really must do? Could we outsource this? Could we abbreviate this process? Does the process and product require all these steps? Could we eliminate doing this task altogether?

"Giving your people different lenses to think through is an excellent way of creating incremental innovation. So, in essence, the lenses cover automating, outsourcing, modifying, and elimination parts of or entire processes. Did you get all that, Sophia?"

"I think so, Ben. Can you check my notes?" Sophia turned the notebook to Ben, and Ben read through the steps of automate, outsource, abbreviate, eliminate and bobbed his head in acknowledgement.

As Ben shifted the notebook back in front of Sophia, he reached for his empty coffee mug almost as a habit. When he held it to his lips, he remembered that he had told the dealer "no more coffee".

"Sophia, we have talked about scenarios where you did role playing. It is a powerful tool to use with your team and yourself because it gives an opportunity to practice something new in a safe environment, rather than out on the floor with real customers. For instance, let's talk through a scenario at The Diner using one of the four lenses. The coffee machine is located in the back of the kitchen. We could abbreviate that process by moving the coffee machine up front behind the counter. Think through how things would be different. Do you suspect the process would be better or worse if you were to make that move?

"Think of it much like the game of chess. You need to consider the ramifications (both positive and negative) of every move. You also need to consider it from your perspective as well as the person you are playing against.

"Even when you are winning, there is value in analyzing and reconsidering everything.

We talked about offering milkshakes. Although they are selling well, it is essential to always be thinking about change and improvement. What isn't selling as well now since we have added milkshakes? If something is selling less, do we need to offer that product anymore? Are certain flavors of milkshakes selling more than others? Are there seasonal flavors we might consider? Could we pre-make something to speed up the process?

"Just asking the questions and thinking through the answers is an excellent way to find improvement. It also makes things more interesting! Let's be honest, this job at The Diner requires using your hands more than your head. This method of role playing and working through potential scenarios engages your team to use their head a bit and not just go through the day like robots."

"Or zombies!" exclaimed Sophia, a closet fan of The Walking Dead, and one of the few still following every episode.

Ben continued, "Once you have the server process written down, you've shared it with your team, and your team is thinking about incremental improvements, you can start documenting other processes. You can document menu items, recipes, the process for ordering ingredients, how to build weekly schedules, how to do a deep cleaning in the kitchen or restrooms. From that, you will find more innovative ways of reducing costs, stress, and preventing fires altogether."

"I can see that now," Sophia said. "Published, visibly-displayed processes in each area that shows each step will help everyone. It is like those IKEA furniture instructions."

Ben replied, "Yes, just make sure they are dynamic and can be easily changed. Some companies publish books or large process maps. What might that say about the process to the employees who perform it? Some may assume that it is set in stone until we print a new one. That being said, some businesses have very efficient and documented processes; the franchise model's success, for example, is dependent on them."

"Like Emanuel's?" Sophia inquired.

"Yes, that is a perfect example," Ben replied. "Adam has very well-documented, tried-and-true processes that the franchisor has provided. From that perspective, he is a few steps ahead of you. He can still do the one percent routine. Rather than focusing on improving operational processes, his people are improving the customer experience and the ambiance.

Ben continued, "The Adjust, Keep it Up, Huddles, Walkabout, Fire Maps, and ClariD's are all universal management tools that every manager should have ready to pull from their toolbox regardless of the type of company managed. The One Percent is a handy tool if you need to make improvements. Both independent companies and franchises can benefit from these tools."

"This all makes a lot of sense to me," Sophia replied. "For now, I want to try and turn The Diner into a franchise. I mean, I want to document and improve the systems, so they are dialed in and repeatable, like at Emanuel's."

"You are absolutely dead on, Sophia! Running any business under the guise of it someday being a franchise is a great strategy. It forces you to focus on a consistent, repeatable experience of quality."

"I think it will be a great way to generate a lot of great Yelp reviews, as well!" Sophia laughed.

"True, Sophia. If you take a look at many front-line type businesses in Yelp, you will see feedback from customers reporting an inconsistent or poor experience. It is common to see one review sharing how the service was excellent, and the next about says the same restaurant was terrible. Overall, businesses are playing off the fact that their average review is good. However, they should be focusing on combating the deviation in outlying bad reviews. My advice to them would be to dig in and really embrace what your customers are saying about your staff and business."

Sophia made a note to herself in her notebook and then looked at Ben.

"I need to make a note to check our reviews and really identify and understand in the poor ones."

"Perfect," replied Ben. "Sophia, do you feel better equipped today than a few weeks ago?"

"I feel so much more prepared to manage! Sophia said excitedly. "I feel like this is doable. This is easy if I follow the system. I know the tasks I need to do as a manager, and I have a system to follow. I feel really empowered. I feel like I have learned more about business in these last weeks than in the previous years of college."

Ben replied, "What you learned in the last weeks was practical and tactical knowledge."
Ben paused for a moment and looked directly at Sophia. She, in turn, knew the routine and locked eyes with Ben as he proceeded. "The better you swim, the less likely you are to sink."

"I like that. I need to write it down. 'The better you swim, the less likely you are to sink.'" Sophia jotted it down in her notebook as a reminder to improve continuously, not just The Diner, but herself.

Ben continued, "Like swimming, management takes practice. You can't just look at your notes and know everything. Much like an athlete or a singer or dancer, practice makes permanent. Look for opportunities to practice with your team. More importantly, practice in a private, safe setting as well, where you can role play, make mistakes, and get better at managing."

"That sounds great, but where do I find a place to practice in a safe environment? Just go over it in my head?" Sophia inquired.

"That can work," Ben replied. "I would recommend finding a group of your peers, like Adam, Aubrey, and others like you. Adam and Aubrey lead a small group that gets together on a video call once a week to practice using the tools. They help each other with the system. They challenge each other and hold each other accountable for practicing with the tools. Most helpfully, they break out into small groups and role-play scenarios with each other. There is even talk of an app."

"Oh, wow! Do you think they would let me join?" Sophia asked.

"I am sure of it. Aubrey texted me earlier to ask if you knew enough of the systems to participate on their calls. Check your phone when you get back to your office. Aubrey may have already sent you the date and time for their next call."

"That would be great, Ben. I feel like I know what I am doing. But, having a group that could help me and teach me would be great."

"The group is outstanding," Ben interjected. "I sometimes jump on the calls, but for the most part, those using the system the longest are helping other newcomers like you."

Anna stepped up to the counter. "Excuse me, Sophia. The sign people are here."

"I am sorry, Ben. I have to run. This has been so helpful. I will make sure to keep you up to date on my progress when you are here at the office. Thank you so much for everything."

"Of course. Anytime, Sophia. By the way, are you getting a new sign?" Ben asked inquisitively.

"Oh, yes! The old one is coming down today and being replaced by a new one! It reads …"

"The Diner—Great food, fast!"

The Frontline Manager's Playbook

Principles

- *Accountability is an invisible force that will manage for me.*
- *Make people aware of the optimal outcome, and they will align their actions to that outcome.*
- *SOPs, or Standard Operating Procedures, must be dynamic and easy to follow.*
  - ☐ *If working for a franchise, the assumption is the process is excellent. Focus on managing the people.*
  - ☐ *If not a franchise, make sure to think like one. Create great processes, and let people follow and improve it.*
  - ☐ *Don't worry about the process being perfect. Get started and tell your employees to find ways to improve as you go along.*
  - ☐ *Always try and seek out deviation. A good system has none. Customers deserve a consistent experience.*

A Frontline Manager's job is to:

1. *Remove barriers*
2. *Provide resources*
3. *Develop people*

To do that successfully, I need to create an environment of accountability and put it to work for me. To do that, I need tools.

The tools to implement accountability and run the system are:

Tool 1: *The Adjust*

I see ..., I hear ..., I understand ... (specify the undesired behavior)
Explain the consequences (what is the ripple effect of this specific behavior)
Help me understand ... (give me your perspective)
Moving forward, what will you do? Look for an "I will" answer.

Note to Self: To be unclear is to be unkind.

Tool 2: *The Huddle*

- *Everyone stands up.*
- *Be brief. (5-10 minutes)*
- *Ask a specific question about success and improvement.*
- *Look for barriers you can resolve.*

*Mini-huddles are OK, too. Just do it!

Tool 3: _The Walkabout or Position to Notice_

Twice a day, step away from my work and walk around with the intention of engaging with your environment and employees.

- _Pick up things._
- _Look at things._
- _Make sure to ask questions._
- _Look for ways to use The Adjust and The Keep it Up._

Remember, people only <u>respect what you inspect</u>.

Tool 4: _Fire maps_

Fires are a metaphor for business challenges that cause you to drop everything and focus all your efforts on solving them.

To stop fires from happening:

1. _Make a map of the work area._
2. _Mark the location of fires on a map with a pin or marker. Look for patterns._
3. _Put out fires, but do not stop there._
4. _Fix whatever caused the fire so that it never will happen again._

Tool 5: _The Keep it Up_

Tell my people what they are doing that you want to see more of, and be specific:

151

1. *I see, I hear, I understand that you ... (specify the desired behavior)*
2. *Explain the positive ripple effect of that action (how it benefits the customer, coworkers, the business, etc.)*
3. *Genuinely acknowledge your appreciation for (specify the desired behavior).*

- *A 3 to 1 praise-to-correction ratio is the target.*
- *Set a goal each week, and make sure you praise each employee at least one time.*

IMPORTANT: Mom's advice for only saying nice things does not apply to management. Be clear, and be honest. Telling people how they can improve is the most helpful thing you can do for them.

Use The Keep it Up <u>weekly</u> with <u>every</u> employee.

Tool 6: <u>The ClariD's</u>

Any time you delegate, or are delegated a project, make sure all four Ds are covered.

- *Who is the Delegated accountable party?*
- *Has there been a clearly Defined expected outcome?*
- *Is there Deadline for completion (a date and time)?*
- *Is there an interval for a regular status upDate on the progress?*

If not, then ask for those things, or provide them before I accept accountability for the request or project.

If I am delegating to others, I must provide them all of the ClariD's. Otherwise, they cannot be accountable.

IMPORTANT: People do not make mistakes. If people can't follow the system, it isn't because they are stupid or ignorant. It is because my system needs improvement. Any time that someone does something incorrectly, I need to first look at my system and find the weakness in it.

Tool 7: _1% Better Every Day_

One percent improvement every day for a year equals a 3,800 percent improvement

Challenge myself and my team to find incremental improvements every day with everything we do. Don't look for the big things. Those take too long and cost too much. Focus on the small stuff.

Think about process from four different angles.

1. Is there a way to automate this?
2. Is this something we really must do? Could we outsource it?
3. Could we abbreviate this process, could we make it more efficient? Even by as little as 1%
4. Could we eliminate doing this altogether?

***My Motto: "Incremental improvement equals
exponential results."***

*Practice the tools. Management is the practice
of managing. Practice makes permanent. Always
remember the better you swim, the less likely you are to
sink. So, use the tools every day to get the best results.*

Epilogue

What you just read was an entry point into the AMP System of Management, which is comprised of tools and content that are as easy to understand as they are to implement.

Think about the methods you are using right now and replace them with these proven tools and compare the results. If you do this "find and replace" method, we know you will see the immediate impact. But remember, practice makes perfect.

Some tools, like The Huddle and Fire Maps, can be modified to some extent to fit your situation. Others, like The Adjust, The Keep it Up and the ClariD's, are designed to work exactly as explained.

To learn more about AMP, its tools and methods, and for additional resources, check out www.ampyouroutcome. com and find links to our books, content, and weekly office hours to ask questions and receive answers live.

Finally, check out the companion to this book, Be A Frontline HERO, which is specifically designed for supervisors and managers with little experience in management.

Derrick & The AMP Team
info@ampyouroutcome.com

Made in the USA
Middletown, DE
17 June 2024

55907963R10089